Giovanni Fanelli

BRUNELLESCHI

Scala/Philip Wilson
Distributed by Harper & Row, Publishers

Contents

© *Copyright 1980 Scala Istituto Fotografico Editoriale, Firenze*
Translation: Helene Cassin
Design: Leonardo Baglioni and Giovanni Fanelli
Photographs: Scala, except nos. 26 (E.C.A.), 27 (L. Rossi), 28 (Cesare Capello S.p.A., Milano), 50 (G. Fanelli), 127 (Alinari)
Produced by Scala Istituto Fotografico Editoriale
Lito Terrazzi 1985
Printed in Italy

Filippo Brunelleschi was born in Florence in 1377. He was the son of ser Brunellesco di Lippo di Tura di Cambio Bacherini, whose family was from Ficarolo on the Po, and of Giuliana di Giovanni Spini. Filippo lived all of his life in a house belonging to the Brunelleschi family in the heart of the old town, behind the church of San Michele Berteldi (now San Gaetano), near the Piazza degli Agli. The house was destroyed in the 19th century when parts of the center of Florence were demolished. Filippo's father was a notary and a diplomat and had a political and economic status of some importance.

We know nothing of Brunelleschi's life before 1398, when, at the age of 21, he was admitted as a goldsmith to the Silk Guild. Little is known again until about 1418, the date of the competition for the model of the dome for the Cathedral. From this time on, documents and contemporary and later sources provide information about his activities and interests. This recorded information, together with the evidence derived from his works, has led to the recognition of Brunelleschi as a man of "universal" genius. According to Manetti, his biographer, he was "an architect, mathematician and excellent geometer, as well as a sculptor and painter." We know that he invented various machines for constructing buildings (he utilized his goldsmith's knowledge of clocks and bells which functioned with multiple gears moved by counterweights); he was a military, naval and hydraulic engineer; he made projects for theatrical performances and musical instruments; he studied Dante's *Divine Comedy,* and achieved a deep understanding of its structure and significance.

The earliest works by Brunelleschi known to us are goldsmith work and sculpture: parts of the silver altar in the Cathedral of Pistoia; the group representing the angel Gabriel and the Virgin of the Annunciation for the Porta della Mandorla on the Cathedral of Florence (Ragghianti); and the relief panel of 1401. These works already reveal Brunelleschi's personal conception of the relationship between figures and space, which led him to break away from the elegant, rhythmic and self-contained equilibrium of Gothic sculpture in favor of a more dynamic conception in which form creates its own space. Despite Brunelleschi's evident mastery of sculpture, sculpture was either excluded entirely from his architecture or strictly subordinated to it. At the same time, his sculptural sense is clearly manifested in the strength and importance of his ribs, cornices, capitals, etc.

In the years 1420 to 1446 Brunelleschi single-handedly created a new architecture, proceeding from his experience of Classical, Romanesque and Gothic architecture and utilizing his own personal solution of the problem of perspective, conceived as knowledge "per comparatione" (Alberti). His achievement appears all the greater if we consider that very few of the buildings which he planned and began were actually brought to an advanced state of construction or completed before his death. The fact that his architectural ideals were recognized and acclaimed, despite the many alterations and distortions of his intentions, is due, as we shall see, to the qualities of unity and universality which characterize his conception. His work marked a decisive moment in the history of architecture and urban design in general, and in the relationship between the artist and the community. Whereas in the Middle Ages the works of Giotto and Arnolfo di Cambio were the fruit of "participation" or rather "delegation" by the community, Brunelleschi rejected these principles, although he had to contend with them. Instead he developed his own personal ideas and anticipated the future with his revolutionary vision of universal significance.

Brunelleschi's works were conceived for an urban context — Arnolfo's medieval town — whose fundamental dimensions had already been definitively established. Indeed, the outer perimeters of the city had been defined, and a dome for the Cathedral had been foreseen by Arnolfo. Brunelleschi's reconstructions of San Lorenzo and Santo Spirito could be interpreted as "modern" versions of medieval ecclesiastical buildings and Piazza Santissima Annunziata as a cloister transformed into a piazza. But Brunelleschi's structures, considered both as units and in their reciprocal relationships, created a new articulation of medieval Florence based on rational, geometric order. Moreover, this order organized not only specific areas within the city, but also the city as a whole with respect to its surrounding territory.

Brunelleschi conceived the city as a new rational entity in which everything, even the past, took on a new meaning. A new kind of city-planning became possible: articulated, yet unified and ordered according to a rationally planned hierarchy, and logical in every part. Far from ignoring the medieval city,

3

1. Works by Brunelleschi in Florence.
Far from ignoring the medieval city,
in fact, taking it as his starting point,
Brunelleschi re-cast the entire preceding
tradition in terms of a new vision
which inverted and profoundly
changed its significance.

I: Extant works certainly by Brunelleschi;
II: works by Brunelleschi which are
no longer extant; III: attributed works;
IV: works no longer generally attributed
to Brunelleschi by modern scholars.

1. Reordering of the house of Apollonio
Lapi in Canto de' Ricci (1409),
Via del Corso (now Grandi Magazzini
'48') / 2. The Schiatta Ridolfi chapel

in fact, taking it as his starting point, Brunelleschi re-cast the entire preceding tradition in terms of a new vision which inverted and profoundly changed its significance. In this sense, Brunelleschi's project for a piazza facing the river for Santo Spirito was an example; the church was no longer seen as the central point in the surrounding urban disorder, but as the focus of a radical reorganization of the quarter within the total urban context. (Compare the role of Santa Croce, in its urban context, with that of Santo Spirito or other works by Brunelleschi). In the medieval town the river, for example, had only a functional role, which concerned separate and independent stretches of it. Instead, Brunelleschi thought of the river as a major structural axis (Manetti speaks of his idea for a port for boats coming from Genoa). It is really due to the work of Brunelleschi that Florence, although it is still basically medieval, has been considered a Renaissance city ever since the 15th century, when the humanists looked on it as an example of the ideal city.

Although Brunelleschi's proposals for urban restructuring remained incomplete and did not lead to a total renovation, it was his approach and that of the Renaissance artists who followed him, including the great architects of the 16th century, which determined the urban form of Florence for the following centuries. Brunelleschi's determining role can be seen, for example, in the peculiar characteristics of Florentine Baroque, in the use in various periods of Brunelleschi's design for the Pitti Palace, in the mirror-image doubling of the loggia of the Foundling Hospital, in the interpretation by Michelangelo and later artists of the modular cube of the Old Sacristy.

Brunelleschi's contribution, and that of the humanist culture of the 15th century, was the result of the critical, interpretative and creative efforts of an élite which can be considered "the first artistic avant-garde in a modern sense" (Argan). Their achievements were more than a "response" or a solution to the demands of the social structure and the system of production of the late 14th century, whose needs could have been satisfied within the ample dimensions of the existing urban structure. "His (Brunelleschi's) architecture lends prestige to the middle class, but it also represents a menace because it implicitly goes beyond the expectations of the mercantile classes. Although the game is now played on a level which the imagination of the lower classes can no longer immediately grasp, the flow and continuity of the existing communication cannot be interrupted too abruptly without compromising the very stability of the institutions; the conservative policies of the Medici, who backed Michelozzo and his followers, are clear evidence of this point." (Sica)

Since there was no necessity, from a social or structural point of view, to elaborate a general plan for the whole city, Brunelleschi imposed his vision of a new urban structure through the characteristics of his individual works; these were invariably conceived on an urban scale and related to an overall urban system.

This also helps to explain Brunelleschi's aim, evident in all of his works, to achieve a balance between longitudinal and centrally planned structures. (This problem had been implicit to some extent in medieval Florentine architecture.) The problem was not, of course, to blend two traditional solutions, but rather to give equal value, in the spatial organization of any structure, to these alternatives: development along a single axis or convergence on a single point. In the Old Sacristy Brunelleschi adopted a plain cube as the basis for his design. In the dome of the Cathedral Brunelleschi sought an equilibrium between the nave of Arnolfo and Talenti and the pointed form of the dome. In the Foundling Hospital the rhythmical, longitudinal development is attained by the repetition of a modular unit consisting of a domed cube. The problem was not to invent a different spatial solution for each different site and function; instead, accepting the diversity of site and function as a point of departure, the aim was to find a solution which, ideally, could be identical everywhere.

Brunelleschi's concern for urban design coincides with one of the central, structural problems of all his work: the relationship between interior and exterior.

The study of Florentine medieval architecture was of primary importance in Brunelleschi's development. Even his use of Classical architecture cannot be fully understood without considering the influence of the local architectural tradition. Many of Brunelleschi's early works are clearly connected to this local tradition: for example, the two perspective drawings of the Baptistry and

in San Jacopo Sopr'Arno (1418) / 3. Work on the Palazzo di Parte Guelfa (documented from 1418 to 1430 and from 1442 to 1458) / 4. The Barbadori chapel in Santa Felicita (1418) / 5. The Barbadori house in Borgo San Jacopo / 6. Dome and exedrae of the Cathedral (1418-46), revetment, galleries and lantern of the dome unfinished at Brunelleschi's death / 7. The Foundling Hospital in Piazza Santissima Annunziata (1419-46); Brunelleschi is mentioned in documents between 1421 and 1426 / 8. The Old Sacristy in San Lorenzo (1419-28), completed before Brunelleschi's death, and the basilica of San Lorenzo (collaboration of Brunelleschi in c. 1425), unfinished at Brunelleschi's death / 9. The Pazzi Chapel at Santa Croce (perhaps begun in 1429; dated on the left wall 1442) / 10. Rotonda of Santa Maria degli Angeli (1434), work left unfinished and completed in the 20th century / 11. Santo Spirito (projects, 1428; work begun, 1436), unfinished at Brunelleschi's death / 12. Palazzo Pitti (work begun after Brunelleschi's death, between 1450 and 1465 / 13. Palazzo Busini, later called Palazzo Bardi-Serzelli, in Via dei Benci, attributed to Brunelleschi (Sanpaolesi) / 14. Project for the rebuilding of the Badia; attributed to this project is a small chapel with cupola of herringbone structure, discovered by Sanpaolesi / 15. Palazzo Quaratesi in Via del Proconsolo; the attribution to Brunelleschi is generally rejected / 16. The second cloister at Santa Croce; the attribution to Brunelleschi is generally rejected. It may have been built by B. Rossellino according to designs by Brunelleschi / 17. Project (not adopted) for Palazzo Medici near San Lorenzo / 18. Work at Palazzo della Signoria; not identifiable.

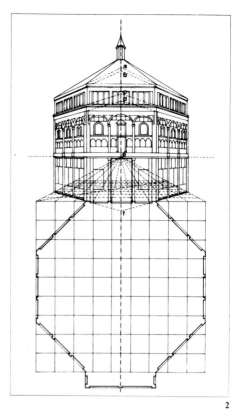

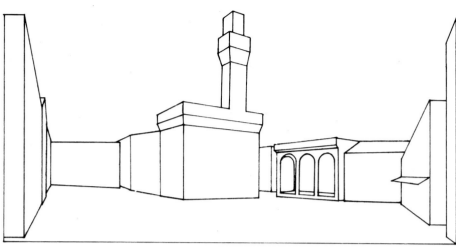

2-3. *Schematic reconstructions of the two perspective panels by Brunelleschi representing the Baptistry and Palazzo Vecchio (according to Parronchi and Ragghianti, respectively).*

4-6. *Cathedral of Pistoia, sculptures by Brunelleschi for the silver altar of San Jacopo:* Prophet *(in quatrefoil frame),* Evangelist, Saint Augustine.

7-8. Sacrifice of Isaac, *gilt bronze panels (45×38 cm.) made by Ghiberti and Brunelleschi for the competition of 1401 for the second bronze door of the Baptistry (Florence, Bargello).*

9. Sacrifice of Isaac, *detail of the panel by Brunelleschi. The interaction of forces and movement brings the story to life.*

7

8

9

of Palazzo Vecchio. His study of these two buildings was essential to the formation of his personal architecture. But the main feature of Florentine medieval architecture, which makes it unique in Italy, is its Classical inspiration. Brunelleschi was familiar with this local tradition, but he refused to work within it; his search for "perfection" led him to seek direct knowledge of Classical models (his trips to Rome are described by Manetti, although they are not documented). Through his study of Classical architecture Brunelleschi formulated certain fundamental principles of spatial organization: first, the use of standardized elements and their assembly, which implies the possibility of repeating the same elements in different structures, changing only the way in which they are ordered (a concept which was the opposite of the Gothic tradition); secondly, the use of the orders to regulate the relationships between the parts; finally, the use of measurement as an abstract concept by which the whole may be unified. Previously, each category of craftsmen (stone-cutters, carpenters, masons) that worked on a building used its own system of measurement (different measures for fabrics, liquids, etc.); with Brunelleschi, everything became subject to the same unit of measure, the *braccio*, which signified an important technological advance.

This way of thinking also explains how Brunelleschi conceived of the city as a unified whole built up of measurable parts, and how he was able, within a span of only 10-15 years, to design and initiate the construction of almost all of his works contemporaneously. In fact, Brunelleschi's artistic career should not be described in terms of stylistic evolution, but rather in terms of the study and elaboration of a recurring problem through parallel experiences.

The vitality which characterizes all of Brunelleschi's works derives from his intense meditation on the relation between form and structure. The way in which the profile of each element projects out into the world, to become part of it and to create and to claim its own space, becomes a matter of vital and even philosophic importance.

A new relationship between the design and its realization also derives from Brunelleschi's basic architectural principles. Traditionally, the architect coordinated the skills of various specialized work groups. With Brunelleschi, a new situation evolved, in which on the one hand, there was an individual "inventor," the architect, and on the other hand, manual workers who carried out instructions according to his design. This relationship sheds light on the conflicts which arose between Brunelleschi and the work-force.

Brunelleschi's conception is taut and clear. His aim was to achieve control of a rational spatial structure, which was completely logical in every part, and in which order and equilibrium would result from the proportional relationships between these parts. His fundamental aspiration was to reduce all elements to an absolute, so that each element would become the perfect realization of its germinal idea; to give finite form to infinite space. Brunelleschi pursued his ideal through the use of perspective. Fundamentally, perspective introduces a central point towards which all elements converge in a logical sequence. It organizes the directional energies, determines the points of equilibrium, requires that equal intervals separate equal elements; it establishes absolutely all measurements and proportions, and orders the dynamics of vision. But visual perspective could order and control architectural space only by ignoring plastic values. For this reason Brunelleschi reduced the architectural structure to perspective lines and planes (even the curved elements are stricly calculated in accordance with the overall perspective scheme); and on the other hand, the material substance was reduced to the white plaster of the wall surfaces and to the lines in grey *pietra serena* of the structural design. Brunelleschi's conception results in the realization of pure space — a rational architectural structure composed according to a perspective calculation and expressed by elements which are conceived two-dimensionally.

In Brunelleschi's conception there is no natural space which *contains* architectural space — instead, the component elements, through their reciprocal relations and their position in perspective with respect to the observer, create their own architectural space.

Argan, in an exemplary analysis, has demonstrated the meaning and importance of the two bronze relief panels made by Ghiberti and Brunelleschi in 1401 for the doors of the Baptistry. The competition was held during the time when Florence stood alone against the armies of the Visconti of Milan, who had already subdued all of the other Tuscan communes. The Wool Manufacturers' Guild, sponsor of the competition, attached greater importance

10

10-12. *Geometry and structure in Florentine Romanesque architecture. Details of the exterior and interior of the Baptistry. Cf. figs. 68-70.*

11

12

than usual to the realization of this work under these conditions.

Seven artists, including Niccolò di Pietro Lamberti, Jacopo della Quercia, Ghiberti and Brunelleschi, participated in the competition. The basic requirements were the same for all: the size and shape (the same as those of the doors by Andrea Pisano which were to be replaced by the new ones), and the subject, which was the Sacrifice of Isaac.

Brunelleschi, who was then 23, had acquired experience as a goldmsith and as a sculptor (the silver figures for the altar in Pistoia), but above all he had studied mechanics (watch-making, etc.). This last activity has been rightly associated with his "inventions" for the construction of the dome. Ghiberti, who was 20, was an accomplished artisan and a painter.

Ghiberti worked slowly, gradually perfecting each detail; Brunelleschi worked rapidly and assuredly. In Ghiberti's relief, the time and place in which events occur remain unspecified; the diagonally placed rock, which separates the two groups symmetrically, places an element of the landscape in the center of the composition and attributes equal importance to the two scenes. In Brunelleschi's panel both time and place are unified and specified, and the triangular composition culminates at the apex in the most important moment in the action. In Ghiberti's work, Abraham's gesture is hesitant, the angel is still far away, Isaac has not taken fright and the ram is still on the mountain. In Brunelleschi's relief, Abraham's gesture is purposeful and contrasts with that of the angel; all elements of the composition participate in the action, which dramatically progresses from the unawareness of the shepherds to the ultimate climax. In Ghiberti, interest in the story and description prevail; in Brunelleschi, everything is seen in terms of the conflicting forces which determine the actions of man as the protagonist of history. In Ghiberti, form is created by flowing lines and nuances and movement dissolves in a luminous space contained by the limits of the frame. In Brunelleschi the form is hard and compact, the action creates its own space, and breaks through the frame (Argan).

The competition was won jointly by Brunelleschi and Ghiberti, to whom equal merit was attributed. Inevitably, Brunelleschi refused to collaborate; the two conceptions were irreconcilable.

The Dome

Brunelleschi must have begun working at Santa Maria del Fiore by 1404, when he was appointed to a committee formed to advise on the construction of the buttresses of the tribunes of the apse of the Cathedral. In 1418 a competition was announced for models and designs for the construction of the dome. Brunelleschi as well as Ghiberti and other engineers and architects participated. As no winner emerged from this competition, further studies were made. In 1419 Brunelleschi received payment for a brick model without armature (Manetti), which he had presented together with Donatello and Nanni di Banco. In 1420 Brunelleschi, Ghiberti and Battista d'Antonio, the director of the project, were nominated to supervise the construction of the dome.

The construction of the dome had to conform to the previously adopted plans for the Cathedral. Work on the Cathedral, begun in 1294 according to the project by Arnolfo, had undergone various vicissitudes, and fundamental modifications of the original plan had been made under the direction of Francesco Talenti when work was resumed in 1357. The dimensions and the form of the dome, its height, width and curvature, had been definitively established in a decree of 1367; whoever continued the work was obliged to respect these specifications. A ratio of 2:1 had been established between the total height of the dome and the diameter of its base, in accordance with the modular system of the entire Cathedral. Between 1410 and 1413 the octagonal drum was built, increasing by about three meters the previously established height. At this delicate moment of junction between the pre-existing construction and the subsequent vertical rise of the dome, Brunelleschi's intervention may have been decisive (Ragghianti). Since the time of the Pantheon no domes of this size had been built. Practical experience was lacking, and faith in structures of this kind had been shaken when the dome of Hagia Sophia in Costantinople collapsed in 1346. And in 1400 the Florentines had had to reinforce the Baptistry which gave signs of weakening.

The building of a wooden armature and centerings of the dimensions necessary for the dome, such as the other competing architects, including Ghiberti, had proposed at the time of the competition of 1418, would have created enormous technological, technical and financial problems. Brunelleschi, instead of reverting to earlier solutions, invented a new technique derived from his knowledge of Roman masonry and eastern medieval architecture. The importance of Brunelleschi's contribution to the realization of the dome consists essentially in the application of a great mind to the resolution of a problem which had already been determined in its basic aspects. The fundamental ideas which guided the solution to the various technical and figurative problems were the rejection of the use of centering and the creation of a double shell. The technique which Brunelleschi devised for building the dome without armature consisted basically in laying the stone or brickwork in rings, in which vertical, integrating elements are inserted to create transitions between the successive horizontal rings (also important was the use of bricks of different shapes, which help to solidify and integrate the circular and radial structures). This technique made possible the creation of the dome as a self-supporting structure. In short, Brunelleschi realized that "while having to build a dome which would appear to be a (Gothic) canopy vault, it could actually be built as a (Roman) arch rotated in 360°" (Di Pasquale). The herringbone procedure (of Islamic origin) was used by Brunelleschi for the vaulting of his other works, and was described in detail by Leon Battista Alberti in his treatise on architecture. It became popular in Tuscany during the first half of the 16th century. The construction of the dome was also greatly facilitated by the numerous machines which Brunelleschi invented to serve in the actual work of building.

Brunelleschi's technical and formal innovations made it necessary to depart from the traditional way of organizing the work of construction. The architect alone became responsible for the project, and the workmen were only expected to carry it out. This revolutionary approach to the relationship between the architect, in his new status, and the workmen, who were assigned an absolutely subordinate role, explains the conflicts which Brunelleschi had with the Opera del Duomo (the Board responsible for the construction of the Cathedral), with Ghiberti, with the workers, and which are recorded in many documents and biographical accounts. The role which Brunelleschi appropriated was in sharp contrast to the corporative approach. In 1434 Brunelleschi refused to pay taxes due to the Guild of Stonemasons and Woodworkers (he was sentenced to jail, and was released through the intervention of the Chapter of the Cathedral). Initially, as we know from documents (see the above-mentioned election of 1420), the construction of the dome was to be carried out under the direction of a committee. But in fact, this original organization gave way as work proceeded and as Filippo's new technical and technological conceptions gradually prevailed. Vasari, who based his account on Manetti, intentionally made a point of justifying Brunelleschi from an ethical point of view; he made it appear that the task had originally been assigned to Filippo alone, and only later to a committee, which had proved necessary only because certain powerful people, seeking to disguise their envy as concern about how to proceed with the work in the event that Filippo should be disabled or die, had exerted pressure on the members of the Cathedral Board.

The successive phases of this exceptional undertaking are described in Manetti's biography with a dramatic intensity that cannot be ascribed only to a preconceived desire to create a myth. In truth, the account is all the more convincing in a writer who made every effort to produce a biography according to the standards of humanist scholarship: Brunelleschi is in Florence in 1417; he is summoned by the workers of the Opera del Duomo to expound his ideas for vaulting the dome — he arouses interest, but also doubts; he then asks permission to leave Florence, and he returns to Rome where he again studies the vaulting techniques used by the ancient Romans, with no regard for his expenses "because he had the construction of that church in Florence continually on his mind"; in 1419 he is once again in Florence and is called to take part in the committee for the building of the dome; he alone maintains that it is possible to build a dome without armature and centerings; the discussion

On the following pages:

Brunelleschi's architecture and urban design in views of Florence from the 15th to the 19th centuries.

13. *Sandro Botticelli, detail of the Crucifixion, c. 1500-05 (Cambridge, Mass., Fogg Art Museum).*

14. *View of Florence from beyond the Porta a Pinti, end of the 15th century (from Bernardino, Le bellezze e casati di Firenze, n.d., c. 1500).*

15. *View of Florence (the so-called Carta della Catena) between 1471 and 1482. According to Ragghianti, this style of representation reflects developments which followed Brunelleschi's perspective panels, and was repeated almost without variation in a series of later views which it inspired.*

16. *View of Florence in the 16th century. G. Vasari: The Seige of Florence by the Imperial Army in 1529-30 (Florence, Palazzo Vecchio, Hall of Clement VII, 1561-62). Cf. fig. 22.*

17. *View of Florence in the 16th century. Axonometric view from Monte Oliveto, by Fra Stefano Bonsignori, 1584 (125×138 cm.).*

18. *View of Florence in the 18th century. G. Zocchi: "View of Florence from the Capuchin monastery in Montughi" (in Scelta di XXIV vedute... published by Zocchi, 1774).*

19. *View of Florence in the 18th century. G. M. Terreni, detail of a view of Florence from Bellosguardo (Florence, Museo di Firenze com'era).*

20. *View of Florence in the 19th century. E. Burci: panorama of Florence from the southwest (Rusciano). Burci emphasizes the interrelationships within the urban structure as well as the relation of the city as a whole to the surrounding hills and to the plain.*

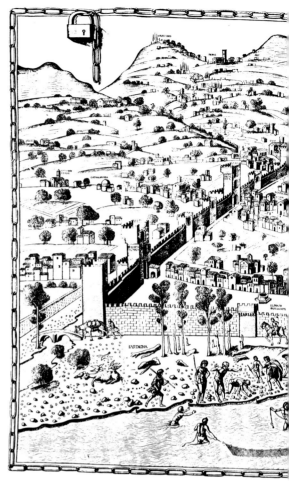

13

14

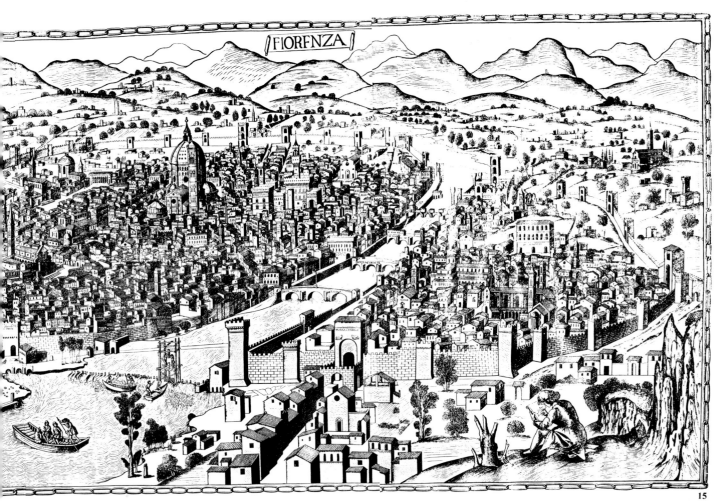

15

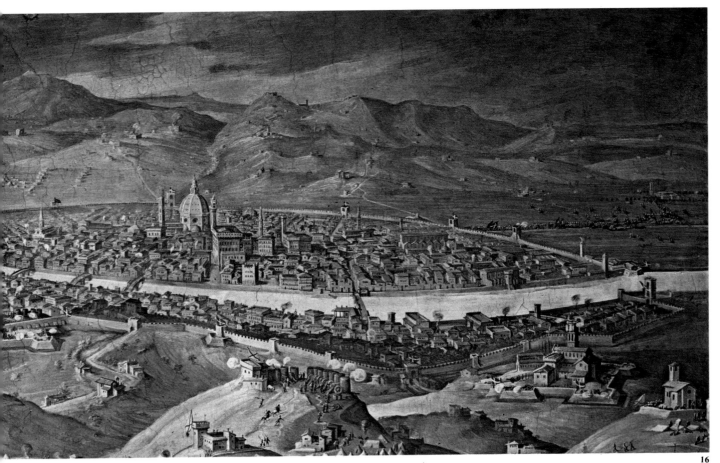

16

13

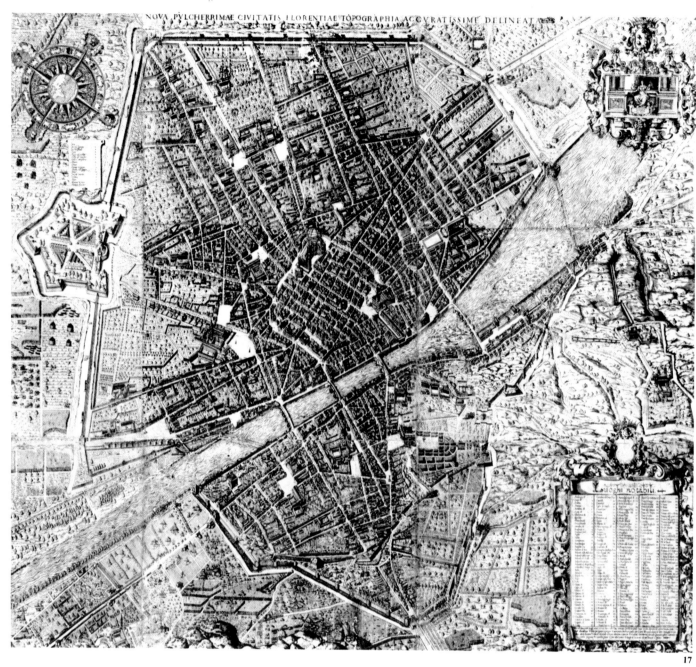

NOVA PVLCHERRIMAE CIVITATIS FLORENTIAE TOPOGRAPHIA ACCVRATISSIME DELINEATA

17

18

19

20

15

21

22

23

lasts for days; the members of the Opera del Duomo, irritated by his obstinate insistence on a seemingly absurd idea, "have him physically expelled several times, as though he were senselessly reasoning with ridiculous words"; he builds the Ridolfi Chapel in the church of San Jacopo Sopr'Arno to prove the validity of his hypothesis; he formulates a program for the construction; he is appointed Master of the Works; he agrees to a lower fee and accepts the limitation of the height at 14 *braccia* as a trial in order to cut short further discussion; he agrees to share the appointment with Lorenzo Ghiberti; he makes a wooden model of the dome; he is called "governor of the great dome," like Ghiberti; but Brunelleschi alone is also called "inventor"; work on the vault is begun according to his instructions; fear and opposition increase; then, pretending to be ill, he demonstrates that Ghiberti is incompetent and that his own personal presence is indispensable; in this way he achieves a division of responsibilities between himself and Ghiberti; he builds new models; he is surrounded by onlookers, which he complains about, and tricks are played on him; when the construction reaches a height of 7 *braccia*, he obtains the commission for the completion of the whole dome and of the lantern; he is requested to assign a "maestro di cazuola" (master mason) to each of the 8 faces of the dome; he ends a strike of workmen, who refuse to be completely subordinated to him, by threatening to continue work with new workers who have been trained by him; he devises various "ingenious measures and precautions" to deal with various possible problems in the construction (wind, earthquakes, the weight of the building itself): he continually makes models of details which he explains to the workmen, using soft earth, wax, wood, and even large sliced turnips; he takes measures to protect the workmen from dangers "and not only real dangers but even the fear and discomfort of the masons and their assistants" and he arranges "that bread and wine be sold on the site and that food be cooked" on the dome in construction, in order to save working time; he personally inspects all of the materials; the organ-

21-22. *Florence and its surrounding territory. Views of the city from the south (from the depression between Via San Leonardo and Erta Canina) and from the east (above Candeli). From whatever distance we look at the dome, as long as it is visible, it presents the same precise form defined by lines and surfaces.*

23. *View of Florence from the Forte di Belvedere.*

17

24. *Brunelleschi's works in the urban landscape seen from within the city. L. Garibbo: panorama of 360 degrees from the Acciaioli tower in Borgo Santissimi Apostoli (1865).*

24

25

25. *Florence and its surrounding territory.
View from the south (Arcetri). In the
foreground: the hills to the south
of the city; in the background,
mountains and hills between Monte Morello
(left) and the slopes of Fiesole (right).*

26

ization is perfect and the work is completed. Even from this brief synthesis of the story of the dome, Brunelleschi appears not as an architect who works within the medieval idea of "participation" or "delegation" from the community — but as an individual who interprets the collective will through the power of his personal vision.

Brunelleschi chose a revolutionary solution for the dome's construction: he refused to imitate the earlier model; he created a form which was of the highest significance in its contemporary context, but which respected the existing buildings: the Cathedral of Arnolfo and Talenti, Giotto's Bell Tower, the Baptistry and the entire city as it then existed. We must attribute to Arnolfo and the Florentine architects of the 14th century who continued the construction of the Cathedral (Francesco Talenti in particular) the merit of foreseeing and preparing the basis for a dome of unprecedented dimensions. We will probably never know whether Arnolfo or the architects who followed him in planning and enlarging the Cathedral had imagined what kind of dome to build and *how* to build it. However, it would not be altogether unreasonable to attribute to Arnolfo and to the culture of his time the courage to plan a construction which would be completed centuries later by other men and with other means which they foresaw would exist in the future as a natural development of the great accomplishments of the present; and to have faith in an idea (the enormous dome) without studying the technical difficulties involved, in the certainty that these would eventually be overcome. Such an approach would clearly have been contrary to Brunelleschi's totally rational planning. In any case, we know from Manetti that a century after Arnolfo, in the discussions concerning initiating work on the dome, the members of the Opera del Duomo expressed the opinion "that this construction was so big and in such a state that it could not be brought to completion, and that it had been naive of earlier masters and of whoever else had deliberated on the matter to have given credence to it." They arrived at this judgement by reasoning in conventional terms (How could the dome be centered?); whereas Brunelleschi resolved the problem through his unique ability to conceive of a totally new and revolutionary approach to designing.

Brunelleschi's contribution to the actual realization of the dome is evident if we compare his finished work with the version represented in the fresco in the Spanish Chapel (Cappellone degli Spagnoli) in Santa Maria Novella. We immediately notice the difference in the proportions of Brunelleschi's structure with respect to the rest of the church and to the city, the different character and quality of the ribs, etc. How did Brunelleschi achieve a new formal conception while respecting the previously established dimensions? Brunelleschi accepted the basilican construction consisting of the nave and two side

27

27. *The Cathedral in the old center of Florence. Aerial view (photo L. Rossi).*

aisles leading up to the octagonal crossing with its tribunes; he rejected the outward-expanding tendency of the tribunes which contrasted with the longitudinal movement of the nave and aisles. Instead, he gathered together beneath the dome these diverse parts of the fabric with their different dynamic movements, reducing them, both in the resolution of the exterior masses and in the interior spaces, to elements participating in a structure which is articulated yet unified and balanced. In other words, Brunelleschi transformed into proportional terms a building which had been conceived solely in terms of dimensions (Argan). The exterior reveals very clearly the distance which separated Brunelleschi from his Gothic predecessors: he rejected the multiplication of vertical, upward-pushing forces (free-standing pinnacles, etc.); he rigorously strove for the convergence of these forces, insisting on a monumental synthesis of continuous lines and surfaces without adhering to the smaller scale of the structure below.

The visible surfaces of the double-shell dome correspond exactly to the

21

28

28. *Aerial view of the dome in the context of the religious center of Florence.*

29. *The dynamics of the dome, "magnificent and swelling" (Manetti).*

28

internal and external spatial organization. In the interior, the basic function of the dome is to coordinate empty space. The vault segments form sharp edges where their surfaces are joined. The rotating surfaces repeat and coordinate the various spatial movements expressed by the nave, aisles and octagonal crossing, coordinating all of them with the vanishing point situated in the empty, receding space of the lantern, which is strongly emphasized by the articulation of the members. The profile of the dome vertically balances the longitudinal space of the nave. "Even today, entering from the doors of the façade and walking towards the crossing, one is struck by the difference between the initial and the final impression: when one stands in the nave, the area of the dome seems like a distant background, far removed from the 14th-century piers and vaults; whereas standing beneath the dome, the area of the nave and aisles is in turn seen as though it were far away, and it assumes a lesser importance, almost like that of the tribunes, so that the structure seems to be centralized around the enormous octagon" (Benevolo).

The basic function of the exterior is to coordinate the volumetric masses. The vault faces are diaphragms stretched between the powerful ribs which converge towards the lantern; the lantern in turn converges towards the great ball which supports the cross. "Another dome must be built over the first one, to protect it from humidity, and so that it would appear even more magnificent and swelling...".

In short, the vault acts as a sensitive diaphragm between two spatial entities, held taut by the pressure of internal and external forces. The thrust

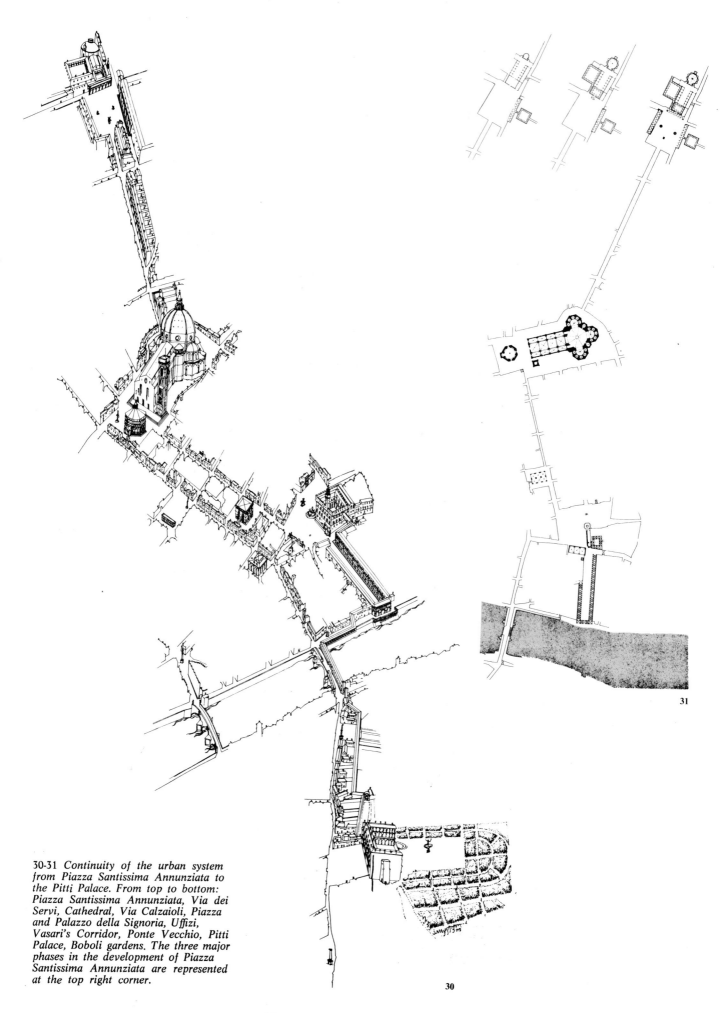

30-31 *Continuity of the urban system from Piazza Santissima Annunziata to the Pitti Palace. From top to bottom: Piazza Santissima Annunziata, Via dei Servi, Cathedral, Via Calzaioli, Piazza and Palazzo della Signoria, Uffizi, Vasari's Corridor, Ponte Vecchio, Pitti Palace, Boboli gardens. The three major phases in the development of Piazza Santissima Annunziata are represented at the top right corner.*

31

30

and dynamic form are resolved in a calculated equilibrium; the dome seems to hover, suspended, above the city — the result of the equilibrium of all of its forces.

The contrast between the white ribs and the red faces, the angle at which the faces are joined, and the tension created by the linear profiles preserve the dome from all "atmospheric" or coloristic effects. On the contrary, these factors create the impression of a clear, rational structure suspended in a continual equilibrium of contrasting forces. The ribs of the dome and of the lantern, for example, define in a centrifugal and centripetal sense an ideal system of radiating planes; and the double shell expresses the balanced tension between the exterior and the internal space which it contains and to which it gives form. The location and dominating dimensions of the dome make it a central point of reference which appears unified and identical from all points of view and which serves as a parameter of both size and proportion.

The red vault segments and the white ribs, seen at that height and in full light, and in their structural and practical protective functions, correspond to Brunelleschi's typical use of the correspondence between color and structure (as in his use of white plaster for walls, gray *pietra serena* for the carrying structure and the absolute light of the windows).

Both the idea and the realization of the dome depend on Brunelleschi's choice of the profile of the vault surfaces and the way in which these are joined. The problem of establishing the exact profiles of the dome is of major importance because their curvature determines the dynamic charac-

32. *The dome of Santa Maria del Fiore and the cupola of Santissima Annunziata situated at either end of Via dei Servi, seen from Giotto's Bell Tower.*

25

teristics of the structure as well as its general form. Recent studies have not yet provided definitive results, or else they have been carried out only on parts of the overall structure; however, they have succeeded in defining with greater certainty the median section of the faces of the dome (found to be polycentric), while the guide to the execution of the whole structure is the profile, which marks the junction of the faces; and it has been ascertained that this profile was originally defined as an arc of a circle (*sesto di quinto acuto*), which can also be seen clearly in the contemporary drawing by Gherardo da Prato. Corrections of the original profile were only minimal, as can be seen in the documents, and after work was already well advanced. If we take into account the height of the dome and its situation with respect to various viewpoints in the surrounding context — from the ground, the towers, the hills, the plain — we observe that the lantern serves Brunelleschi's intent to negate the material substance of the architectural mass and reduce it to a structure which controls space. (The model for the lantern dates from around 1436; work on the ground was begun in ca. 1438; its assembly was begun in the year of Brunelleschi's death and completed in 1471.) The eight buttresses of the lantern, which intentionally correspond to the ribs of the dome, define the vertical planes which intersect each other along the ideal vertical axis at the center of the dome. In 1432, the question of how to close the dome at the top was debated, and an octagonal ring was chosen. The ribs are connected at the apex of the dome by horizontal pieces which also define the vault faces and constitute a platform. The octagonal lantern rests on this platform, and is conceived as an articulated structure with buttresses which radiate from the central axis. The lantern serves structurally to tie the ribs by weighing on their point of junction. As a formal solution the lantern stresses the point of convergence of all the thrusts, the relationship between mass and space, and between internal and external space. The structure was assembled after a remarkably thorough study of building methods and is made of hollowed-out blocks of marble. Brunelleschi invented special machinery for hoisting the various parts and setting them in position. The monumentality of the elements, conceived for being seen from a great a distance, can be appreciated only from close up. The modulated surfaces of the buttresses and the pyramidal membrane produce chromatic variations which, when seen from below or from a distance, create an illusion of two-dimensionality and incorporeality. Marble and brick, or grey stone and white plaster, which represent Brunelleschi's typical bi-chromatic preference, would not have been appropriate in this case. Here the bi-chromatic effect is achieved by the modulation, the shaping, the hollowing out, etc. of the marble. In full daylight pure white is the only color which can create a sense of immateriality and weightlessness. The lantern is therefore completely successful as a formal structure which radiates and absorbs light, and yet is seemingly without substance (Luporini).

In 1439 work was begun on four small exedrae under the drum of the dome, in the areas which had been used for storing building materials (these areas are still used for the storage of materials and the original building equipment). The exedrae appear as curved surfaces into which large niches, separated by columns, are inserted. The successive concave and convex movements in the exedrae introduce a new articulation of the masses in the area of the apse. The exedrae also serve to balance the large tribunes, which by themselves constituted isolated masses projecting from the octagonal core of the apse. While at first the exedrae seem only to add additional forms to the massing at the apse, in fact they relate primarily to the dome, forming, together with the tribunes, a continuous ring of projecting masses at the base of the dome. In addition, the concave/convex play of their surfaces negates any real sense of mass, and thereby reinforces the apparent weightlessness of the dome which seems to require little support.

The Cathedral and its dome, as originally planned by Arnolfo, indicate the intention to create a structure which would rise above the city-scape, but which would be essentially equal in importance to Palazzo Vecchio, and thus balance it. But Brunelleschi's dome, beyond its importance as a symbol of religious faith and of the power of the Wool Guild which commissioned it, assumes even greater significance as a formal structure which epitomizes the entire organization of the city and its territory. The dome was intended to be more than just "another" great architectural monument; its principle function was to impose a dynamic reorganization of all relationships and by

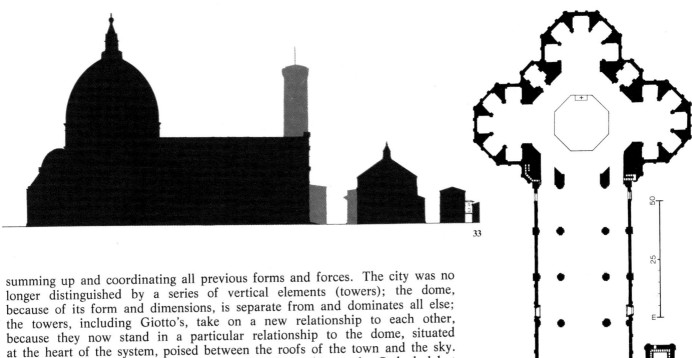

33

34

summing up and coordinating all previous forms and forces. The city was no longer distinguished by a series of vertical elements (towers); the dome, because of its form and dimensions, is separate from and dominates all else; the towers, including Giotto's, take on a new relationship to each other, because they now stand in a particular relationship to the dome, situated at the heart of the system, poised between the roofs of the town and the sky. We must evaluate the dome not only in its relationship to the Cathedral but also with respect to its location in the center of the city in proximity to the Baptistry, Giotto's Bell Tower, etc.

The relationship of the dome to the Baptistry is particularly significant. Despite the differences in function and scale between the two structures, important parallels exist: in the relationship between the elevation and covering, between vertical walls, vaulting, lantern and ball, between plane and mass, and between color and structure in various parts of the two buildings; and in other details as well, such as the planned decoration of the interior of the dome with mosaics (it was decorated instead with frecoes by Federico Zuccari and Vasari in the 16th century). Although a direct visual comparison of the two structures is not possible, we notice nonetheless that they are aligned on the same axis in accordance with an ideal conception which had been planned by Arnolfo but to which Brunelleschi attributed a different perspective value. In one of Brunelleschi's two famous perspective panels, he "sees" the Baptistry from a viewpoint in the central door of the Cathedral — that is, from a particular point on this axis.

A relationship also exists, in terms of formal structure, between the dome and Palazzo Vecchio, despite the obvious differences. The relationships between the solid rectangular mass of the lower block, terminating in the enormous crenellated gallery, the tower, also with a crenellated gallery, the aedicule crowned by an arcade and battlements, and, finally, the cusp which supports the ball and lion; as well as "the dialectic contrast between the weight of the solid mass and the rising thrust in unstable equilibrium, suggesting the existence of an enormous dynamic energy which overcomes the resistance of mass and transforms it into a dream of hyperbolic strength" (Marchini) — these are aspects of Palazzo Vecchio which Brunelleschi must surely have considered.

Alberti gives a superb definition of Brunelleschi's masterpiece in the dedication to his treatise Della Pittura: "rising above the skies, ample enough to encompass in its shadow all the people of Tuscany" ("erta sopra i cieli, ampla da coprire chon sua ombra tutti i popoli toscani"). "Rising above" describes both the tension created by the curved profiles of the ribs and the fact that the dome is not dominated by the surrounding space but rather creates its own space and defines the relationship of all else in respect to itself. The word "ample" expresses the characteristics of extension and circularity of the dome, while "ample enough to" indicates the concept of this structure as a recapitulation of the relationship of the entire city to its surrounding territory. And the balanced contrast between "rising above" and "ample enough to" expresses perfectly the solution of all energies, structures, equilibriums, proportions, technical problems in the absolute abstraction of the dome and in the tension of its profile, etc. In addition, Alberti's description suggests that the

35

33. *The dome in the urban structure: the religious center. Longitudinal section of the Piazza del Duomo and the Baptistry before the Archbishop's palace was moved further back.*

34. *Plan of the Cathedral of Florence.*

35. *Section and exterior view of the dome (C. von Stegmann, H. von Geymüller). Note the horizontal walkways between the two shells on four levels: the first at the base of the dome, two intermediate levels and the fourth level at the base of the lantern. Cf. fig. 45.*

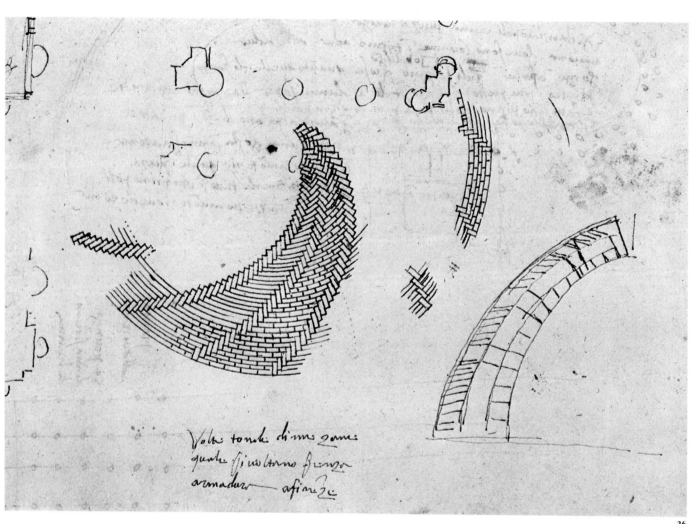

Volta tonda di mezane
quale si voltano senza
armadura — a fine

36

37

38

new size of the dome corresponds to the new political dimensions of the city.

Due to the character of the medieval plan of the city, the dome never dominated the view from the streets. Indeed, it can be seen from only a few streets which enter into the Piazza del Duomo (Via dello Studio and Via dell'Oriuolo, which was widened in the 19th century) and from some parts of Piazza Santa Croce and Piazza del Mercato Vecchio. It is significant that the only street where the dome is a dominant visual factor is Via dei Servi at the end of which Brunelleschi built the Piazza Santissima Annunziata. The dome can be seen best from a height — from the upper floors of the buildings, from the towers or from vantage points beyond the limits of the city walls. Only in this way does "the view from afar determine its unity and its relationship to the profile of the surrounding hills and to the sky" (Ragghianti) — and only from a distance is it possible to compare the dome to the other major monuments to which it is related. This "distancing" from the immediate context and the definition of those viewpoints from which the dome is endowed with an objective unity is present in all of Brunelleschi's works and in those inspired by his thought. For example, from the Via Romana we look up at the Pitti Palace, raised above the level of the piazza: if we enter the portal, pass through the building to the courtyard and turn around to look down towards the houses, these appear to lack foundations and seem to be suspended above the street, their roofs at the horizon; and the tower of Santo Spirito appears on the main perspective axis. In a similar way, the platform of the loggia of the Ospedale degli Innocenti (the Foundling Hospital) is situated at the horizon line if viewed from the square; on the other hand, the square appears "distanced," objectified, when seen from the

36. *Drawing attributed to Antonio da Sangallo the Younger (Uffizi, Gabinetto dei Disegni), showing the procedure used for constructing "rounded vaults in brickwork which in Florence are built without armature."*

37. *Walkway between the two shells (second level, see fig. 35): Passage area in corrispondence to an angle rib between two vault faces. Note the curved lines at the intersection of the rib with the outer shell (at the right) and with the inner shell (at the left), and the herringbone masonry.*

38. *Detail of the herringbone masonry at the fourth level (at the base of the lantern, see fig. 35). At the right is the jamb of the access to the stairs of the third level walkway (fig. 42). The oculus opens onto the space between the inner and outer shells (see fig. 41).*

39. *Interior of the exedra on the east side. Work instruments, dating from the fifteenth century and later: tongs (10), set of stone-engaging keys or hangers (11), and various types of pulleys.*

29

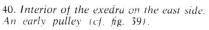

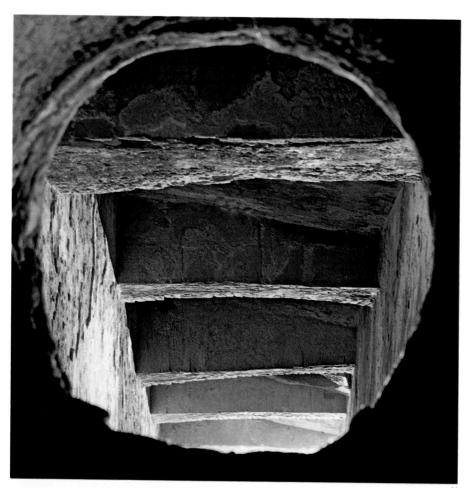

40. *Interior of the exedra on the east side. An early pulley (cf. fig. 39).*

41. *Small curved buttresses between the ribs of a vault face (cf. fig. 45), seen from above through an oculus on the fourth level (at the base of the lantern).*

42. *Space between the inner and outer shells: flight of stairs connecting the third and fourth levels (cf. fig. 35), carved out of the inner shell and enclosed at the sides by the intermediate ribs of the vault face.*

43

44

43. *Space between the inner and outer shells: flight of stairs leading from the second to the third level walkway. To the right is the extrados of the inner shell; to the left, the intrados of the outer shell (three "small" or arcuate vaults can be seen).*

44. *Space between the two shells, extending between the median ribs (seen at right and left) of a vault face. The outer shell can be seen at the top, with an oculus at the center which opens onto the exterior. (View from the second level, looking upwards).*

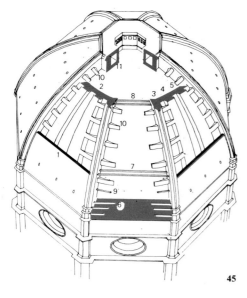

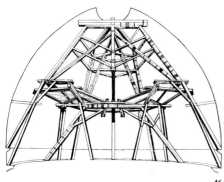

45

46

45. *Drawing showing the structure of the dome: 1. outer shell / 2. inner shell / 3. angle rib / 4-5. intermediate ribs / 6. non-elastic stone chain at the lower level / 8. non-elastic stone chain at the upper level / 9. elastic wood chain / 10. "small" vaults (reinforcing elements which connect the angle ribs to the intermediate ribs) / 11. closing ring of the dome and base of the lantern.*

46. *Scaffolding used for vaulting the dome without armature (G. B. Nelli, 1775).*

47-49. *The dome seen in natural light: morning, midday, afternoon.*

50. *The dome in the cityscape. View from the top floor of a house on Via de' Pandolfini (photo Fanelli).*

On the following pages:

51. *The dynamics of the ribs and faces of the dome.*

52. *The relations between the exedrae the drum, the dome and the lantern.*

53. *Model in wood of the lantern (Florence, Museo dell'Opera del Duomo).*

54. *The lantern seen from Giotto's Bell Tower.*

55. *A window of the lantern from the exterior, detail.*

56. *The buttresses of the lantern.*

57. *The buttresses of the lantern and dome, seen from the cusp of the lantern.*

height of the loggia. And again at Santo Spirito and San Lorenzo Brunelleschi created this same effect: viewed from the rest of the city, these structures are abstracted and isolated on a higher level; yet the view from the level of the churches makes the rest of the urban structure (squares, streets, etc.) seem abstract and objectified.

The dome is indeed very large, but its great size produces a very different impression from that of Gothic cathedrals, which tend to "draw in" the spectator from a close-up view and which, from a distance, seem to merge with the atmosphere, to blend with nature. The concise and dynamic form of the dome attracts and gathers together the forces and lines of vision which converge upon it and radiate out from it again. But from far away it retains, by means of its profile and the relation between ribs and vault segments, its quality of just measure; it thus constitutes, from whichever point one views it, a form which is perfectly individuated and self-contained and which determines all proportional relationships within the visual field. *From whatever distance we look at the dome, as long as it is visible, it presents the same exact form defined by lines and surfaces.* We frequently find place names throughout the Florentine countryside such as "Apparita" or "Apparenza" (apparition): these names point to the fact that from the locality thus named the city can be recognized or, rather, it's existence implied, by the emergent profile of the dome.

In studying Brunelleschi's dome many of Alberti's writings take on a particular meaning. For Alberti (in *Della Pittura*), "All visible things are nothing but surfaces"; surfaces have certain "constant" qualities, "l'orlo e il dorso" (that is, contour and plane), and other variable qualities "due to variations of site and illumination."

Since it is far higher than all other Florentine buildings, the dome is subject only to the conditions of natural light, whereas the light in the streets and squares is affected by the reciprocal relationships among the buildings. The typical alternation of light and shadow on the dome's faces during the course of the day is due to the curvature and texture of its surfaces and to the profile and projection of the ribs; yet these variations in its illumination parallel those in the streets and squares, since all are dependent on the movement of the sun. In this way the progressive movement of shadow on the surface of the dome articulates, moment by moment, the variation of light and shadow throughout the city, which is conditioned by the direction and form of the streets, the space between buildings, and other factors.

It was no accident that Toscanelli, a friend of Brunelleschi, created the first sun-dial using the dome as a perfect instrument. Through an opening in the lantern a ray of light crosses the space of the dome and falls on the dial on the pavement below. We do not know exactly what the original illumination of the interior of the dome was like.

The function of the dome as an emblematic and coordinating structure, and as a module of proportion, was immediately perceived by the first "modern critics," Alberti and Vasari. And Manetti recognized the "absolute" significance of the dome.

The size of the dome is commensurate to the plain enclosed by the hills surrounding the city, and it was built with materials taken from these hills. Entire quarries were set aside to be used only on its construction. And Vasari observed that "the hills surrounding Fiorenza appear similar to it."

Although precedents for all of the elements of the dome may be found in earlier architecture (the pointed shape, the ribs, etc.), the result is an unprecedented form, an ideal creation, which became the symbol of the life of the community and its surroundings.

The double-shell dome creates a viable space inside the structure, constructed "in such a way that one can walk between one and the other" (Vasari). This means of access was essential to the workmen during the construction. We have already noted that kitchens were set up so that the workmen did not have to leave the site for meals, thus saving valuable time each day; and Brunelleschi, during the construction, lived in a house at the foot of the dome.

This walkway between the internal and external shells is still accessible; in order to climb to the top of the dome, one enters into this interior space, follows the original course of construction, and shares in Brunelleschi's exalting experience. For Brunelleschi's total dedication to the project, so vividly described by Manetti, went beyond the technical requirements of the job: "And then he went to the ironmongers for various and diverse objects in

47

48

49

50

33

51

52

53

55

56

58

59

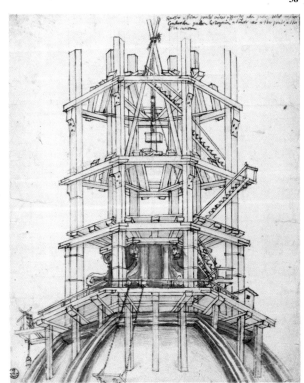

60

38

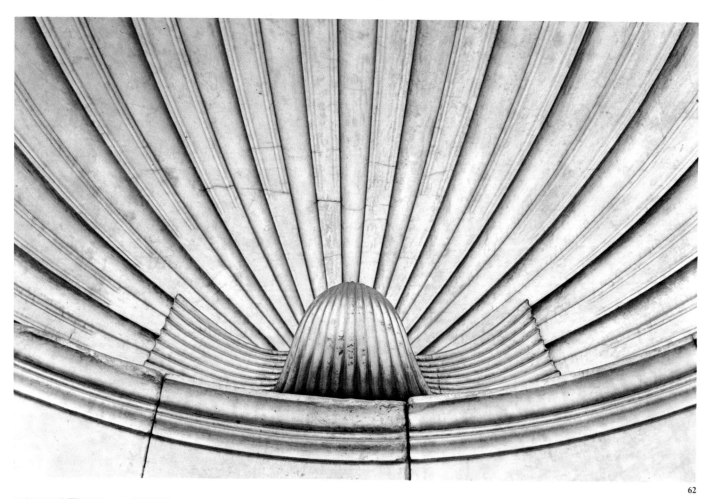

62

63

40

iron which even the craftsmen had difficulty in understanding. And then he went to the joiners with new methods and new conceptions and provisions for various kinds of objects which no one else would have imagined, and lights for use in areas in climbing up and down and avoiding bumps or falls in the dark. And he wanted to avoid all shocks or danger, and not only danger but even fear and discomfort for those who had to go to these places. And since the masters and apprentices, who paid their own expenses, would not lose time, he arranged for cooks to be there and for bread and wine to be sold to those who did not come prepared, so that the workmen would have everything they needed and no time would be spent in idleness... There was not a small stone or brick which he hadn't checked to see if it was in good condition and well-fired and cleaned: something which no care was expended on afterward, since today attention is paid only to what appears to be economical, and stones from the river and rough bricks and all sorts of crudity are employed. He used wonderful care in mixing mortar, and he went in person to the brickyards regarding the stones and the baking, the mixture of sand and lime, and anything else that was required. He seemed to be a master in every field."

64

65

The Foundling Hospital

Work was begun on the Foundling Hospital, which had been commissioned by the Silk Guild, in 1419. Brunelleschi's name appears on the documents relating to the construction only until 1427. The building was inaugurated on January 25, 1445, although the stairs were not completed until 1457. The project was modified during the course of construction, probably to enlarge the complex. According to Manetti, who was a member of the committee responsible for the construction in 1466, the most important changes that were made increased the length of the façade and also altered the design of important compositional elements — the frieze, the architrave and the entire composition of the upper story. The design of the interior recalls the Hospital of San Giovanni Battista, founded in 1388 by Bonifacio Lupi, and the Hospital of San Matteo (now the Accademia di Belle Arti) founded by Lemmo Balducci. But with Brunelleschi, hospital architecture (in this case it is not really a hospital but a home for abandoned illegitimate children) was given an importance equal to that of other major religious and secular buildings and became a major component of the urban image.

The idea of a portico may have been derived from the porticoes of classical squares, as well as from 14th-century Florentine loggias such as those of Piazza della Signoria and Orsanmichele, with pointed arches, or from the loggias of the hospitals of Lupi and Balducci. In the case of the Foundling Hospital, the loggia is not conceived as an independent unit; it obeys the same laws which govern the whole building and the surrounding urban context. Moreover, it characterizes the first Florentine square to be conceived as a unified structure, and to be "planned" by a single mind (the side of the square realized by Brunelleschi determined the form of all later additions — the loggia by Sangallo and Baccio d'Agnolo, the fountain by Tacca, the statue by Giambologna). Brunelleschi's design is based on clear lines and planes and is calculated to create a sense of spaciousness (the square is designed to appear larger than it really is). The square is situated in front of the old church of the Servites, at the end of the Via dei Servi, a "new" street which had grown up in the 13th and 14th centuries and which Brunelleschi transformed into a major axis between the Cathedral and the new, symmetrical square.

Brunelleschi exploited the natural conformation of the area (a depression created by the waters of the Mugnone which had flowed through here at an earlier time), by raising the sides of the square onto platforms with high steps, and by decreasing the importance of the accesses from the other streets. He

58. One of the ribs, seen from the platform of the lantern.

59. View of the interior of the dome and of its octagonal drum from the level at the base of the lantern.

60. Gherardo Mechini: drawing of the scaffolding for the construction of the lantern (Uffizi, Gabinetto dei Disegni).

61. View of the interior of the lantern.

62. Detail of one of the niches of an exedra.

63. An exedra.

64-65. Details of the cornice and paired capitals of an exedra.

66. *Plan of the Foundling Hospital complex (F. Bruni, 1819).*

67. *Frontal view of the façade of the portico of the Foundling Hospital.*

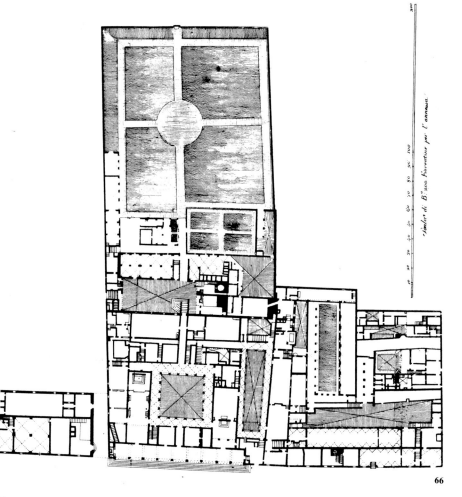

66

clearly intended the square as a world-in-itself, isolated, unitary and perfect, and related to the rest of the city by a single artery, the Via dei Servi, which functioned as a "telescope" aimed at the dome of the Cathedral (which a few decades later corresponded in turn to the dome of Santissima Annunziata).

The level of the platform of the loggia itself is at eye level for an observer standing in the square. The arcade should not be seen in terms of a potentially infinite longitudinal extension, but as a self-contained repetition of identical modular units. The interaxial distance between the columns is exactly 10 *braccia*, and the height of the columns is 9 *braccia*; therefore each bay consists of a cube capped by a hemisphere. This is a spatial module theoretically capable of summarizing the nature of the space of the whole loggia. The loggia is an exterior space in respect to the hospital; it is an interior space when seen from the square because it lies behind the plane of the façade. It creates a subtle solution "by comparison" to the problem of the relation between them. This concept helps us to comprehend the proportions of the module of the columns and the relation between the diameter of the column and the inter-columnar space. The actual material structure of the architecture is limited to the minimum needed to define the exact relationships between the various units of space — the square, the portico, the interior of the hospital. The network of spatial relationships is not defined by the physical structure, which serves only to define its limits. For these reasons the loggia constitutes a space which must be directly experienced. Other indirect means, such as photography, can nevertheless help to interpret some fundamental aspects, such as the function of a plane as a diaphragm, or limit, determined by the exchange between inner and outer space.

Brunelleschi's conception of Piazza Santissima Annunziata also demonstrates his dual capacity for achieving idealized abstraction and organic unity. The raised, deep loggias create a play of light and shadow which reflect the movement of sunlight at different hours of the day and in different seasons in relation to the vast expanse of the square below between the loggias. The roundels, which are a symbolic key to the architecture, were filled in later

69

70

71

72

73

74

75

68. *Detail of the façade of the Foundling Hospital.*

69. *Detail of one of the faces of the Baptistry.*

70. *Detail of the façade of the portico of the Foundling Hospital (cf. fig. 11).*

71. *Portico of the Foundling Hospital: a capital.*

72-75. *Capitals from medieval Florentine buildings: San Pietro Scheraggio, Santissimi Apostoli, Santa Croce, Palazzo Busini-Bardi.*

45

76. *The modular space of the portico of the Foundling Hospital.*

77-78. *Plan and modular section of the Old Sacristy in San Lorenzo.*

79. *Interior of the cupola with "crests and sails" covering the main space of the Old Sacristy.*

On the following pages:

80. *The Old Sacristy in San Lorenzo: frontal view of the wall which opens onto the apse. The two doors leading to the auxiliary rooms, the stucco reliefs above them and the roundels in the spandrels are by Donatello. The altar is by Buggiano.*

81. *Detail of the cornice with angels and grid motif which runs around the exterior of the Old Sacristy and the adjacent Medici chapels.*

82-83. *Details of the articulation of the walls of the apse.*

84. *The dome over the main space and the small cupola over the apse (with the astrological fresco). Notice the linear pattern of tangential circles.*

76

(1463-6) with the glazed terracotta figures by Andrea della Robbia; they were originally intended to remain empty, like the ones in Masaccio's fresco of the *Trinity* in Santa Maria Novella and in the Barbadori chapel in Santa Felicita (Sanpaolesi). Many elements in the architecture of the Foundling Hospital, such as the capitals, impost blocks, extradoses, arcades and architraves, were derived from Florentine Romanesque architecture.

It is difficult to reconstruct Brunelleschi's design for the upper part of the façade, but it has been described in the following way by Manetti when he writes about the mistakes committed by the architects who came after Brunelleschi: "there is another [error] in the two windows and in the small pilasters that were to rise from the [lower] cornice that functions as the sill for the windows up to the [upper] cornice; this [upper] cornice should be where the eaves of the roof are now." The façade would have been similar to that of a cloister. An element of which we know Brunelleschi disapproved was the bent architrave, which is similar to the one in the attic of the Baptistry.

The interior of the Foundling Hospital is also organized according to a highly rational design. The axis of the central bay of the portico establishes a longitudinal axis which runs through the interior and is symmetrically balanced by the long corridors, the courtyard with its portico, the large rooms and the service areas. The dimensions of the main part of the interior are coordinated to the various parts of the façade. Many 15th-century structures, from Michelozzo to Giuliano da Sangallo, were derived from the design of the Foundling Hospital.

46

The Old Sacristy

The Old Sacristy of San Lorenzo was probably begun in 1422 (in the fresco in the dome above the altar the stars are depicted in their position in the sky over Florence on July 9, 1422) and finished in 1428, as we know from an inscription on the lantern. The Sacristy was intended to be the family chapel of the Medici family. The patron, Giovanni di Bicci, who died in 1429, and his wife were buried in the sarcophagus beneath the marble table; and later, the tomb of his grandsons Piero the Gouty and Giovanni were built into the left wall.

The Sacristy is composed of a main square space, measuring 11.60 meters or 20 *braccia* per side, covered by a hemispherical dome on pendentives: and of a secondary space which is also covered by a small hemispherical dome. The elevation of the larger unit is articulated in three zones: the lower zone is defined by pilasters and trabeation; the intermediate zone is articulated by arches along the perimeters of the walls; and the upper zone consists in the dome. The square (cube) and the circle (sphere) as pure geometric forms are the fundamental modules of the spatial organization, as in the loggia of the Foundling Hospital. The spatial structure is created by the interplay of pilasters, trabeation, arches and the ribs of the dome, all made of gray sandstone, which delimit the plaster surfaces. All of the secondary elements — windows, medallions, the framing of the niches in the area of the altar — are placed tangentially with respect to the principal elements, so that their position is clearly defined.

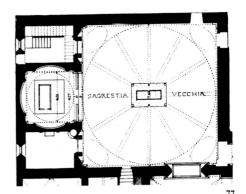

77

In contrast to medieval interiors where all of the surfaces were covered with decorations, here the elements are reduced essentially to two: the linear articulation in relief and the planes of the wall surfaces. The great importance attributed to the ideal geometric forms of the square and the circle, emphasized by the system of linear articulation, and the interplay between the articulation and the plastered surfaces, represent the two fundamental characteristics of the architecture of the Sacristy.

Since the space of the Sacristy is defined by the relationship between the linear pattern of the articulation and the plastered wall surfaces, the dimensions of these surfaces are extremely important (that is, the spaces between the stone elements, excluding the elements themselves). The following observations are of considerable interest: 1) the entablature is the only element which is continuous along the perimeter of the two spaces; 2) since the height of the two zones above the entablature is directly determined by the overall plan (these zones consist of semicircles whose diameter is equal to the length of a side of the room), the height of the lower zone, between the floor and the entablature, is of fundamental importance. If we examine the dimensions of the Sacristy we note that the height of the lower zone is approximately equal to half the length of one wall, all measurements being taken from floor level. Consequently, the height of the main space, from the pavement to the base of the dome, excluding the thickness of the entablature, is practically identical to the length of one wall. To summarize, the height of the lower zone was dictated by Brunelleschi's desire to create a basically cubic space covered by a hemispherical dome; the entablature, and in general all of the horizontal articulation, are composed of elements whose own dimensions are not included in calculating the overall relationship. Againn, as at the Foundling Hospital, the basic spatial unit is a cube surmounted by a hemisphere.

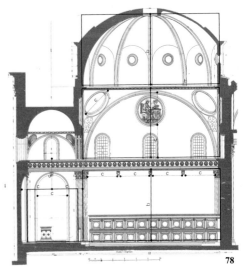

78

This interior further demonstrates Brunelleschi's principle of the circularity of space. The circularity of the dome of the Cathedral is repeated in the various circular elements of the vaulting, the lantern and the ball; here, in correspondence to the four walls of the square, which themselves create a circular movement from one to the other, we find the repetition of the arches, then the dome on its circular base and the round opening of the lantern at the center. Since the walls are close to each other, given the size of the room, they are conceived as planes which intersect the visual pyramid. With respect to the circularity of the plan, the four walls become four projected planes (Alberti: "each plane has its own pyramid"), on which the design of the articulation and the proportions of the walls translate the coincidence of internal and external spatiality. The four large arches above the entablature therefore assume the function of horizontals for each of the four main direc-

79

47

81

82

83

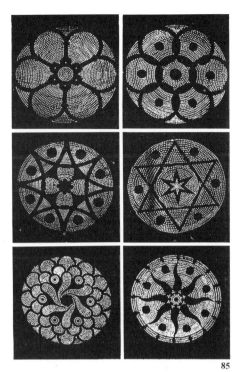

85

86

87

85. *The Old Sacristy of San Lorenzo: designs of the perforated iron discs placed in the openings of the dome to filter the light.*

86. *Remains of the original sloping roof above the small cupola of the apse seen from the space beneath the present covering.*

87. *View from the roof of the transept of San Lorenzo of the covering of the Old Sacristy with its lantern (dated 1428 on the trabeation), restored in 1939-40.*

tions of the space; and tangential to these, the circular base of the dome synthesizes these horizontals in a single, circular horizontal (Argan).

Brunelleschi's architecture in the Sacristy creates a space which ideally represents all possible space; in a similar way, the space of the apse, created by opening one of the walls, reproduces the image of the space of the Sacristy. In other words, the repetition in the apse of the spatial organization of the main space of the Sacristy serves to confirm the equivalence, in terms of perspective vision, between actual depth and the condensation of depth created by the articulation of the walls. In this context the pilasters which embrace the angles of the opening between the two spatial units have a particular function: these are the only complete pilasters in the Sacristy, and they serve to focus one's gaze along the central axis of the wall which opens into the apse. The illumination comes from above, and there are no other openings which create a visual relationship to the exterior; the interior space is an absolute space, which excludes all others.

Light enters through the twelve oculi in the dome so that there is no single source of concentrated light; the round openings, filled with ironwork discs of various designs, filter the natural light and serve to diffuse it in a uniform manner. The original illumination has been modified by the alteration of the area of the apse.

The reduction of the architectural vocabulary to two terms, the dark gray articulation and the white plaster surfaces, diminishes the sense of mass in favor of perspectival illusion. The entire articulation of the interior of the Sacristy expresses Brunelleschi's desire to interpret space in optical and chromatic terms (rather than in sculptural terms), within a perspectival structure. The function of the wall as a diaphragm is emphasized by the use of mensoles under the entablature (a motif taken from Classical architecture); these seem to replace the wall itself in its supporting function, so that it appears as an immaterial surface.

In the overall design no element is independent: each has a function which contributes to the creation of an ideal, perfect perspective space. The roundels, in their basic monochrome definition, are coherent with the overall scheme; but the reliefs are meant to be enjoyed in themselves, and require a close-up view for detailed appreciation. Manetti has recorded Brunelleschi's criticism of Donatello's doors leading to the two rooms next to the apse. Although these doors are beautiful in themselves, they interrupt the perspectival unity of the space of the Sacristy with their pronounced sculptural quality and because they introduce new elements (columns and tympanums) which have no relation to Brunelleschi's structure. Verrocchio, on the other hand, (who contributed to other works by Brunelleschi as well — for example, the ball on the Cathedral

52

lantern) demonstrated a deeper understanding of Brunelleschi's spatial conception in the Sacristy, by giving a strictly linear and chromatic character to his work. In his monument to Piero and Giovanni de' Medici, he scrupulously limited himself to the depth (70 centimeters) of the wall and avoided any projection of the volumes into the space of the chapel. Indeed, he thinned Brunelleschi's wall/diaphragm almost to the point of transparency. Manetti offers a lively account of the interest aroused by the revolutionary architecture of the Sacristy: "... it astonished all of the people of the city as well as foreigners who chanced to see it, for the novelty and beauty of its style. And so many people came continually to see it that it greatly disturbed the men who were working on it."

The design of the Old Sacristy also has a symbolic function. The triadic rhythm, evidenced in both a vertical and horizontal sense, refers to the Trinity, and the twelve segments of the dome, each illuminated by a round opening, symbolize the light shed by the teachings of the Apostles. According to Battisti, the number 4 represents another fundamental symbolic element.

The Pazzi Chapel

The Pazzi Chapel was probably begun in 1429-1430 after the completion of work on the Sacristy at San Lorenzo. The interior was completed in 1444; the dome was vaulted in 1461, according to the inscription on the dome itself; work on details continued during the following years (funds were still being allocated for the decoration in 1478). The structure was intended as a chapter house, with a chapel situated behind the altar where the family of the patron was permitted to bury their dead. In this structure next to Arnolfo's church of Santa Croce, Brunelleschi did not need to construct on a large scale in order to create a perfect and self-contained structure based on a principle of geometrical purity and essentiality. In the interior, Brunelleschi further developed the solution used in the Old Sacristy, and achieved a maximum unity of design. The plan is essentially the same, except that the square space of the main area is enlarged laterally so that it becomes a rectangle. The dome is placed above the central square, while the two short lateral arms are barrel vaulted. The bench which runs continuously around the perimeter of the main space, at a height corresponding to the floor level of the secondary space, was used when the chapel functioned as a chapter house. The stone bench provides a uniform base for the pilasters, which constitute the only articulation of the lower zone of the chapel. The pilasters are contained within the two constant levels defined by the bench and the entablature. The entablature, as in the Old Sacristy, is the only element which continues horizontally around the entire perimeter. The arches above the pilasters create a transition to the dome and follow the inner curve of the lateral barrel vaults. According to Benevolo, "the structure depends on three measurements (two for the plan and one for the elevation) which are independent and which can be expressed in whole numbers," using the *braccio* as the basic unit. It is important here, as in the Old Sacristy, to measure the spaces between the elements. In the Pazzi Chapel the white wall surfaces are emphasized to the maximum so that the chapel seems to irradiate light from within. The length of a side of the square of the main space is identical to that in the Old Sacristy; the side of the apse, however, is longer, so that the interval between the pilasters at the entrance is approximately twice the width of the wall surface between the pilasters which frame the apse and the pilasters at the (imaginary) corner of the (imaginary) square of the main space. This surface in turn is equal to the one next to it which creates the lateral extension of the main area. (The total width was determined by the distance existing between the side of the church and the convent.) In the side walls, which are slightly shorter, this ratio is almost exact. The two short arms, which form part of the overall geometric scheme, also serve to balance the depth of the apse and, on the opposite side, the windows and the door. If we call a side of the square of the main space l, then the height of the pilasters, from the bench to the entablature, is equal to $3/4\, l$; and the distance from the entablature to the intrados of the

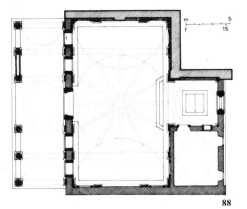

88

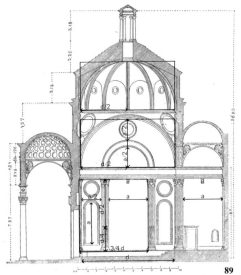

89

90

53

91. *The exterior of the Pazzi Chapel is*
the product of early remodellings
and 19th-century restorations.

92

92. Detail of the façade with modular partitioning of the surfaces.

93. The Pazzi Chapel seen within the precincts of Santa Croce: view from the bell tower.

On the following pages:

94-96. Frontal and perspectival views of the "interior façades" of the Pazzi Chapel.

93

94

95

56

97

97. *Frontal view of the left wall: the architectural space is created by the use of lines on plain surfaces.*

98. *The spatial structure of the Pazzi Chapel seen from the center of the lantern.*

On the following pages:

99. *The system of vaulting in the Pazzi Chapel.*

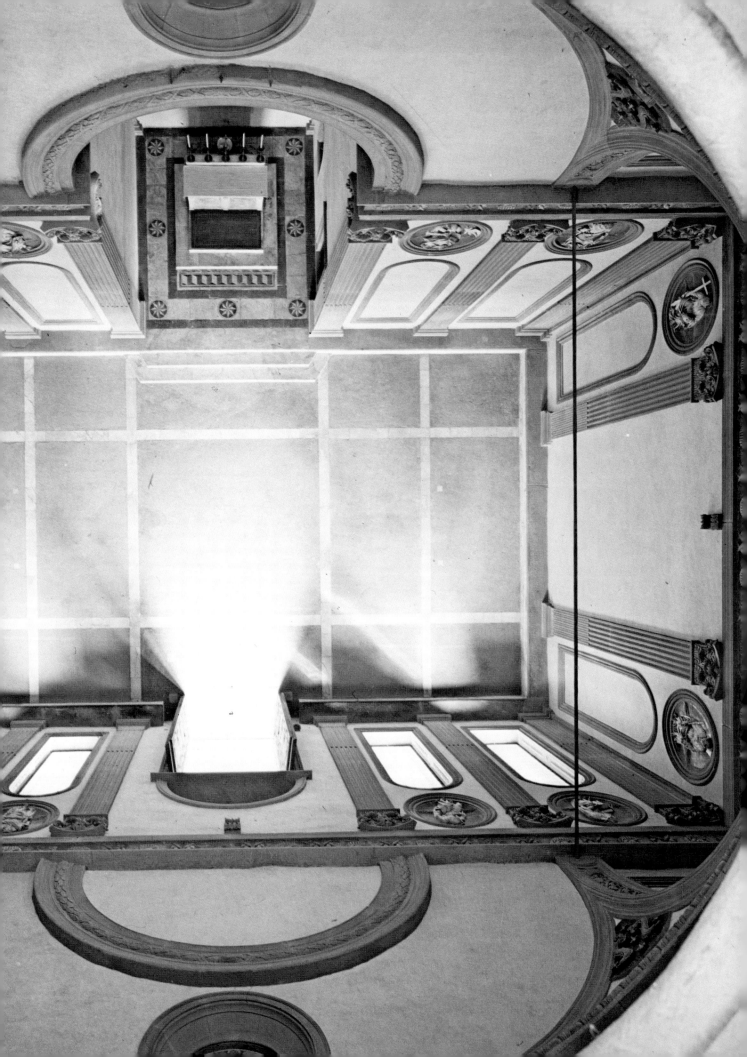

100

101

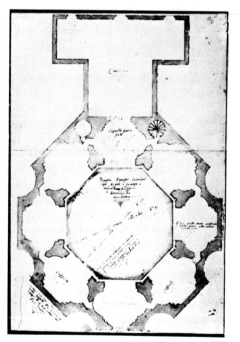

102

103

100-101. *Santa Felicita, the Barbadori chapel: general view and detail of a corner with shafts and capitals of two columns made of single superimposed stone blocks.*

102-106. *The Rotunda of Santa Maria degli Angeli: drawing based on the original plan (Paris, Louvre); details of the interior (the entire revetment was*

104

105

106

107

remade or added in the late 1930's;
only the architrave above the door in
fig. 103 is original); view of the exterior
in a miniature in the Rustici Codex.
(Florence, Seminario Maggiore).

107. Santa Maria Novella, fresco of the
Trinity painted by Masaccio with the
collaboration of Brunelleschi for the
architectural structure designed
in perspective.

63

arch is equal to 1/2 *l* (the ratio between the two measures is 1.5 : 1.) If we measure the interaxial distances, the order (including the pilaster and the trabeation) equals 15 *braccia* and the proportion between the interaxial distance (counting between the corner pilaster and the one adjacent to it) and the height is 1 : 3. The equivalence established between the real depth and the illusion of depth "drawn" on the wall which we already saw at San Lorenzo is also present here, in that the design of the three walls of the main space reproduces exactly that of the fourth wall which opens onto the altar space.

Brunelleschi also treats the light sources as part of this overall geometric scheme, as he had done in the Old Sacristy. The profiles which define the windows on the entrance wall are repeated on the wall surfaces of the chapel, as though to demonstrate that the real spatial profundity is equivalent to that "drawn" on the wall, and that the white wall surface is merely a diaphragm. The portico which precedes the chapel serves to "filter" the light coming in from the outside; in this way the light admitted by the entrance wall merges with the light from the dome creating a uniform illumination. The stone bench around the perimeter of the main area emphasizes the function of the wall as a diaphragm by negating the fact that it rests on the ground. In the same way the wall brackets (beneath the entablature, as in the Old Sacristy) deny the supportive function of the entablature, and, in keeping with the conception of the walls as perspective planes on which the design is projected, the pattern of stone which articulates the tile pavement corresponds to the pilasters, which are the basic element in the organization of the articulation.

The exterior underwent various remodellings after the death of Brunelleschi and in the 19th century. The lantern was "restored" at the end of the last century in an effort to model it on the lantern of the Old Sacristy at San Lorenzo; two capitals from the original lantern are preserved in the Cathedral Museum. We do not know to what extent the portico, which was built after Brunelleschi's death, corresponds to his design.

San Lorenzo

The story of the construction of the new church of San Lorenzo is very complicated, particularly because of the problems created by the existence of the earlier Romanesque structure which was temporarily preserved during the construction of the new church; even modern research has not solved all of the related problems. According to Benevolo, "Due to the circumstances under which the construction took place, San Lorenzo became a sort of experimental workshop where Brunelleschi himself as well as those who came after him proceeded tentatively, testing the adequacy of his methods to deal with the many obstacles and opportunities which arose during the work." On Dec. 12, 1418 the prior of San Lorenzo obtained permission to expropriate the land now occupied by the transept in order to enlarge the absidal end of the earlier church, for which purpose many houses, a street and a small square were demolished. Work on San Lorenzo was begun on Aug. 10, 1421, but it is not certain just when Brunelleschi's intervention began (perhaps around 1425). Work was interrupted many times. As Manetti noticed, the plan recalls those of the churches of Santa Croce, Santa Maria Novella, Santa Trinita and Santissimi Apostoli. The innovation which Brunelleschi introduced at San Lorenzo was the organization of the structure according to a proportional module observable from the central axis of the nave and corresponding to a calculated perspective scheme. The basic geometric unit remains the square. San Lorenzo has three naves which terminate in a transept with five chapels on the far side, of which the largest, the apse proper, is the same width as the central nave, while the other four chapels are the same width as the lateral naves. There are six

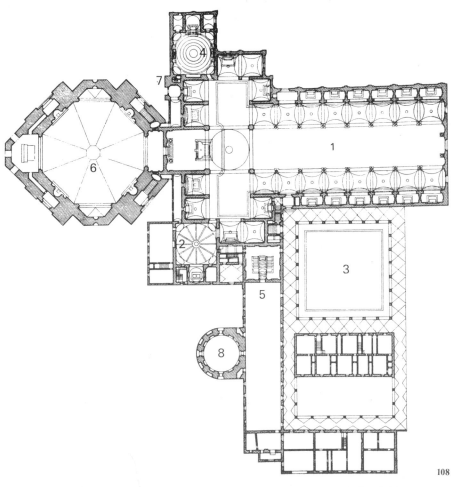

108. *Plan of the church and monastery of San Lorenzo. 1. church of Brunelleschi / 2. Old Sacristy (Brunelleschi 1419-28) / 3. cloister attributed to Michelozzo (after 1457) / 4. New Sacristy (Michelangelo 1520-34) / 5. Laurentian Library (Michelangelo 1523-29) / 6. Cappella dei Principi (Don Giovanni dei Medici, Buontalenti, Nigetti and others, 1605-1737 / bell tower (F. Ruggeri, 1740-41) / 7. Dolcian Library (P. Poccianti, completed in 1841).*

109. *San Lorenzo: axial view the interior.*

108

109

110

111

110. *San Lorenzo: general view of the transept.*

111. *Details of the articulation (abbreviated pilaster) in the corner of a transept chapel.*

112. *Transverse view across the naves: the "measure" of a bay.*

other chapels in the transept (which is the same width as the central nave): two are situated at the ends of the arms of the transept, in such a way as to leave space for the doors to the sacristies and to the two adjacent communicating chapels; the other two chapels in the transept are located on the near side, opposite the end chapels of the far side. There are twelve smaller chapels with barrel vaults which open out from the two side naves; these were added towards the end of the 15th century. It is not clear whether these correspond to Brunelleschi's project, which had provided for a continuous series of chapels like those in the transept, and which would have been closer to the design of Santo Spirito. The articulation of the lower zone consists in pilaster strips (framing the side chapels of the lateral naves and the chapels in the transept) and columns (in the nave); these serve as the base for the covering of the side naves and of the chapels of the transept. The four crossing piers beneath the dome are faced with pilaster strips of greater height and support the trabeation which runs around the entire perimeter of the transept and central nave. It seems as though the major order was imposed on the minor order with the intent of creating an architectural unity between the nave and transept but without taking into consideration the planimetric consequences (Benevolo).

According to a recent hypothesis (Hyman), after Brunelleschi's death, when work was resumed under Cosimo the Elder, construction was continued under the direction of Michelozzo, who was also working on the nearby Medici Palace at that time. The hypothesis is based on the fact that the same workmen were employed on the two projects.

The exterior of the church has masonry with horizontal ribbing. Contemporary sources speak of faulty construction and of abandonment of Brunelleschi's original design and model. In recent "restorations," the plaster facing has been removed. The steps were built in 1915 in imitation of the steps at Santo Spirito.

66

Santo Spirito

The earliest projects for Santo Spirito date from 1428. Brunelleschi thought of reversing the orientation of the church so that the façade would overlook a spacious square facing the Arno. We have already observed the importance which Brunelleschi attributed to the relation between architectural structures and the urban context. The project was never realized because of the opposition of various families represented on the commission which was to approve the project and who owned houses and land in the area between the church and the river. The fact that Brunelleschi's plan was effectively blocked indicates that the power of the citizenry was still strong, and demonstrates the gap which existed between Brunelleschi's architectural ideals and the capacity of his patrons to comprehend and accept them.

In Brunelleschi's original plan for a church facing the river, he probably intended to go beyond the typical medieval relationship of church to square (with the church situated in a corner of the square); but a traditional relationship was ultimately reinstated, and represented another victory of the patron's will over Brunelleschi's intentions.

The main walls of the Old Sacristy and the Pazzi Chapel measure about 20 *braccia* per side, and San Lorenzo and Santo Spirito are approximately the same width. These similarities demonstrate Brunelleschi's idea that every architectural structure ideally is realized by a single recurrent solution.

At Santo Spirito, which Brunelleschi considered closer to his ideal conception, the width of the central nave is exactly double that of the side naves (at San Lorenzo this ratio is only approximated). "At Santo Spirito all of the planimetric proportions are based on the length of one side aisle bay, which measures exactly 11 *braccia*... This result was achieved by designing in multiples of simple units, a method which Brunelleschi had experimented in earlier structures. In this case the module is not the *braccio*, but a larger unit of 11 *braccia* (the interaxis), or else half of this unit, that, is, 5 1/2 *braccia*. All of the principle dimensions of the building are determined by multiplying this unit of 5 1/2 *braccia* by the arithmetic series: 1 (depth of the chapels), 2 (interaxial distance between the columns of the minor order), 3 (height of the minor order and height of the springing of the vaults of the lateral naves), 4 (height of the apex of the arches of the lateral naves and interaxial distance between the columns of the major order), 5 (probable height of the springing of the vaulting of the central nave). The two arms of the Latin cross formed by the central nave are obtained by multiplying the same unit by 12 and by 24, and the two axes of the church by multipling by 18 and 30 (if we imagine that the small chapels would have continued also along the façade, as suggested by Folnesics).

"These comprehensive measurements bear the same relation to each other (2:3:4:5) and were probably obtained by multiplying by a larger module equal to the sum of the widths of the two naves. For this reason Santo Spirito stands as a prototype for compositions based on simple relationships — that is, on an aggregation of equal metrical elements — which Wittkower considers typical of Renaissance culture.

"Brunelleschi's method of designing requires the use of different systems of measurement for different purposes. In this case we can identify at least three of these. One system, used for the overall dimensions of the total structure and its relation to the urban context, is based on a module of 5 1/2 *braccia*. A second system, used for the details of construction, is based on the *braccio*. A third system, used for ornament (mouldings, capitals, cornices, etc.), probably utilizes a further series of sub-multiples. The largest module (5 1/2 *braccia*) and the smallest (1 1/2 *braccio*) are the units which permit transitions from one system to another and give continuity to the whole" (Benevolo).

The errors made by those who continued the construction of Santo Spirito after Brunelleschi "are evidence of the cultural conflict between Brunelleschi and his own generation as well as the succeeding one; his followers made mistakes because they were accustomed to thinking of architectural details as independent of the overall scheme, whereas here they were confronted by a structure in which all details were intimately related to the whole. By the end of the 15th century the more progressive Florentine intellectuals deplored the fact that Brunelleschi's design had been spoiled by those responsible for the construction, and it is likely that the biography of Brunelleschi attributed

114

113. *San Lorenzo: detail of the articulation between a transept chapel and the left nave.*

114. *Detail of a pilaster in the transept.*

On the following pages:

115. *Plan of the church of Santo Spirito. Reconstruction of Brunelleschi's original idea with chapels visible from the exterior along the entire perimeter and the four entrances on the "facade."*

116. *Drawing showing a hypothetical solution for the covering of the central nave and transept with barrel vaults.*

117. *Detail of the articulation between the side aisle and the transept at the base of the cupola.*

118. *Detail of the articulation along the right flank of the interior.*

119. *A bay of Santo Spirito based on the square module which organizes the architecture of the church.*

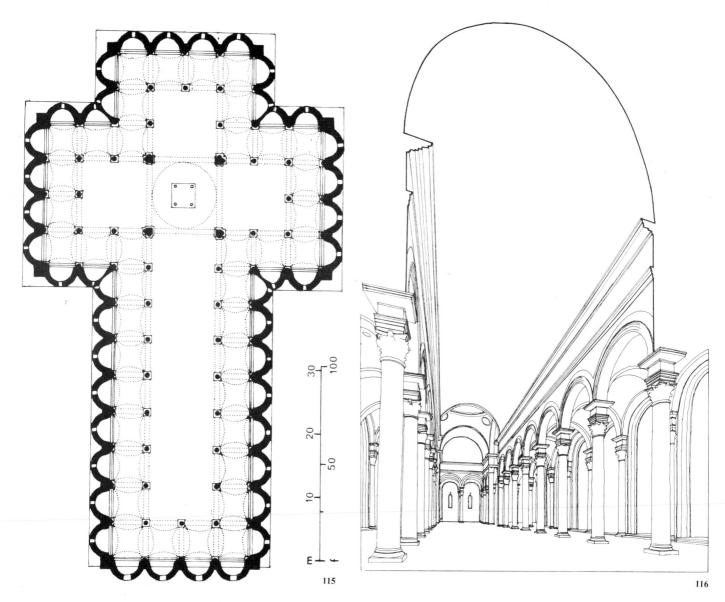

115

116

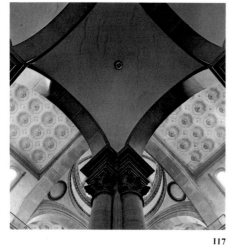

117

118

121

122

123

124

125

126

to Manetti grew out of the debates on this issue. But the results should not be ascribed only to the incompetence or arbitrariness of those who continued Brunelleschi's work; even more important were the changes in architectural ideas and practice which took place in the late 15th century. Although later architects accepted Brunelleschi's revolutionary concepts as their basis, they addressed themselves to different problems, and in particular, to the study of the architectural experiences of the past from which they hoped to derive a canon of structural types and building techniques. The standard of building techniques, no longer considered an autonomous field of study, declined markedly and hindered the invention of new types of structures" (Benevolo).

In Santo Spirito Brunelleschi carried to a logical conclusion his search for a total space in which every part would be differentiated according to its function and yet subservient to a unified conception, a unified organism. Here Brunelleschi attempted to resolve a maximum complexity by means of a repetition of equal parts which are related to a unitary organism — the whole. He strove to realize his concept of multiplicity in unity by determining all measurements by proportions. The articulation of the spaces at San Lorenzo was achieved by the use of pilasters and columnas of varying heights; here, by columns all of the same height. The lateral spaces are no longer perceived as distinct units and in a perspective progression, but are directly connected to the space of the central nave. By using only columns for the articulation and by creating a series of curved chapels, Brunelleschi achieved a perfect solution to the central problem posed in all of his work: the realization of the exterior wall as a plane/diaphragm — the product of an equilibrium of positive and negative movements, of concavity and convexity. All straight walls are eliminated in Brunelleschi's plan, and the continuous alternation of convex and concave surfaces makes it impossible to evaluate the thickness of the outer wall, so that the structures no longer appear as material substance, but only as an articulation of a spatial entity. Moreover, this characterization of the outer wall solves the problem of the relation between interior and exterior by making these identical, as the chapels were intended to be seen from the outside as well. According to Brunelleschi's intentions, there were to have been four chapels on the façade; but this innovation was abandoned by his successors.

The repetition of a single module around the entire perimeter gives form to Brunelleschi's concept of circularity. This overall circularity is reflected in the perimetral wall, in the vaulting of the naves, in the form of the columns, in the mouldings, in the profiles of the windows, etc. The arms of the central nave were probably intended to be covered by barrel vaults. This concept of circularity achieves that unity of longitudinal and centrally planned structures which Brunelleschi had always pursued. "Rather than a programmatic fusion of a centralized and a longitudinal plan, it is an organic transformation of the naves of the longitudinal block into an atrium which runs directly, with no interruption, into the crossing" (Luporini). Another aspect of Brunelleschi's design which demonstrates his search for continuous circularity is the placement of columns in the center, at the extremities of the arms of the cross. In classical art, symmetry makes all elements converge at the center on a point which is also the center of visual focus, with respect to which the lateral extremities are out of focus. Here, in order to achieve equal clarity throughout, the eye is helped to broaden its vision laterally so that all parts of the visual field remain sharp. We can include in Brunelleschi's intentions regarding circularity his unrealized plan of creating four entrance doors in the façade.

At Santo Spirito the column becomes an exemplary structure, an ideal form which creates its own space in the same way that the human figure in Masaccio's art creates its own space (Argan). Whoever enters the church, whether tourist or "sanfredianino" (a resident of the neighborhood of San Frediano), after having climbed to the top step of the platform which raises the church above the piazza, and after having passed through the portal — immediately feels compelled to move and act according to a measure, a tempo, a rhythm which is that established by the architecture. The architectural structure and the ideal space create a particular relationship to the human form. The proportion of the column is such that a moving figure requires a certain time to reappear after it has disappeared behind it. This, too, contributes to the rhythm and manner in which human actions occur within this space. This structure, conceived as a perfect "idea," that is, brought to perfection and complete in itself, cannot be fully appreciated immediately upon entering. It

127

must be experienced by walking through it, absorbing it, and participating in its most vital aspects (structures, objects and people, at various distances and in various functions with respect to the circularity of the whole), at different hours of day and in all seasons. Even the distribution of light, which has unfortunately been altered by various factors (the upper part of the central nave does not correspond to Brunelleschi's design; most of the windows in the lateral chapels are partially or completely obstructed), comes closer than in any other building by Brunelleschi to his ideal of a diffuse illumination which helps to create an abstract, ideal space.

Brunelleschi's design for Santo Spirito is so rigorous that even the unfinished or subsequently remodelled parts, such as the façade and exterior flanks of the nave, retain a particular significance. The exterior of Santo Spirito in relation to the square is still a splendid example of Florentine design. In no other architecture, in no other square, do we feel so intensely the significance of the steps we take to reach the level of the church, and then to enter from the porch into the interior. The scale and number of the steps force us to walk with a rhythm which is identical to the "tempo" of the interior of the church. The platform on which the church stands is not an abstract space, for it is broad enough to serve as a square where children play and old people sit in the sun in the winter, in the shade in the summer, whereas the ordinary, hurried passers-by tend to avoid it. The relative isolation of the church, due to its elevation above the level of the square, is common to all of Brunelleschi's architecture (the dome of the Cathedral, San Lorenzo, Santo Spirito, the Pitti Palace). Brunelleschi's poetic intuition for reorganizing and idealizing medieval urban solutions became, in Alberti, a colder, more intellectual manner of imposing ideas conceived *a priori*. Brunelleschi's structures emphasize the temporal and spatial relationship between the observer and the architecture, and in this sense they are not monumental, whereas Alberti (in Mantua and at Santa Maria Novella) clearly sought effects of monumentality.

128

127. *Piazza Santo Spirito at the end of the 17th century.*

128. *Detail of a corner of the transept from the exterior.*

129

130

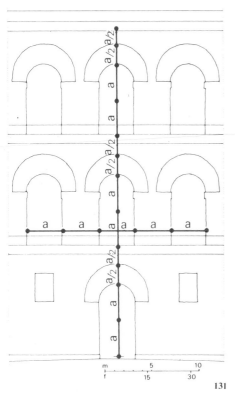

131

129-130. *Palazzo di Parte Guelfa: details of a corner and of the large segmentally arched windows.*

131-133. *Palazzo Pitti: diagram showing the modular organization of the façade (drawing by the author); Brunelleschi's palace in the lunette painted by G. Utens for a villa at Artimino (1615-20); view of the part designed by Brunelleschi, from the bell tower of Santo Spirito.*

132

134. *The pulpit of Santa Maria Novella by Brunelleschi and Buggiano (Andrea di Lazzaro Cavalcanti).*

134

135. *Santa Maria Novella, Gondi Chapel: Wooden crucifix (between 1410 and 1425).*

135

The Palaces

It is difficult to ascertain many aspects of Brunelleschi's activity in the field of civic architecture, nor has this part of this career been sufficiently studied. According to Manetti, Brunelleschi worked on the Palazzo dei Priori (Palazzo Vecchio) where he employed new masonry techniques, but no trace of his work there has survived. Manetti also reports that he constructed the houses of Apollonio Lapi and of the Barbadori family. The former, which was situated near the Canto dei Ricci, still exists in part (Grandi Magazzini "48"), and has octagonal columns and leaved corbels. "The Barbadori house, which is in Borgo San Jacopo at the entrance to the Ponte Vecchio, on the left side, next to the Rossi tower, was in the zone destroyed by the Germans in World War II.

The country villa of the Pitti family at Rusciano has been completely transformed. For the Palazzo di Parte Guelfa Brunelleschi was commissioned to design a new meeting hall and two adjoining rooms. The large hall was built over the structure of the building beneath it which already existed. Several aspects of Brunelleschi's solution recall Orsanmichele: the large arched windows overlooking the city and the oculi, as well as the smooth sandstone surface of the exterior wall, uninterrupted by any articulation. Tradition holds that Brunelleschi made a model of a palace for Cosimo the Elder, which was to have been built "on the square and isolated on all sides" (Vasari), that is, between the Via dei Gori and the continuation of the Via de' Biffi, where later Ammannati's Jesuit monastery was built. Brunelleschi probably planned a structure with a square plan, with nine windows on each side and with the main entrance on the same axis as the portal of San Lorenzo. According to Vasari, Cosimo rejected the project "to avoid envy rather than expense." This was a typical manifestation of Cosimo's political prudence, which consisted in his ability to rule without ostentation.

According to documents, the construction of the Pitti Palace was begun after Brunelleschi's death. Although there is no documentary proof of the attribution of the project to Brunelleschi, its conception is so original that it seems impossible to assign it to anyone else. "Who could change the name of the palace of Luca Pitti? Pitti himself lived there for only a brief period, so that when it became first the residence of the grand dukes and then the royal palace, the name of the original owner could easily have been forgotten. But the effect of the enormous impression created by this exceptional construction remained" (Sanpaolesi).

The design of the Pitti Palace may have been related to Brunelleschi's model for Palazzo Medici. And the use of enormous windows to characterize the façade clearly recalls the Palazzo di Parte Guelfa.

The Pitti residence stood outside of the center of the city and was set back from the main road, where the other principal Florentine palaces were situated. It was built during a period in which a shortage of housing was aggravated by the construction of large palaces. Luca Pitti used his authority with the Signoria to demolish many houses in order to create the new site. The people who were forced to abandon their houses were not given new homes, as remained the case throughout later centuries in similar urban interventions imposed by the ruling classes. Houses were demolished in the Via Romana in order to open the large square, the first to be created for a private palace and the first example of a Renaissance square closed on three sides.

The palace is built on rock, which made it possible to construct an edifice of such exceptional size. The *muraglia antica*, or "ancient masonry" (Vasari, Lapini), is composed of gigantic blocks which must have posed technical problems in quarrying, transportation and assembly. As Taine observed, they are not stones "but parts of boulders and almost sections of mountains."

The palace has three entrances on the square, a solution which may be compared to Brunelleschi's plan for several entrances to Santo Spirito. The use of identical windows on all floors, and the equality of the windows to the doors, represented a total innovation. The design and dimensions of this single element, whose repetition constitutes the design of the façade, had been experimented by Brunelleschi at the Palazzo di Parte Guelfa. The balustrades at the bases of the second and third floors give the appearance of very narrow balconies which continue along the entire length of the façade.

The central arches on the first floor were originally open (see the predella

136

by Allori in Santo Spirito and the Utens lunette as well as the view of the palace in the now detached frescoes from the façade of the Pitti residence at no. 15 Borgo Santo Spirito), and formed a loggia; this original design reappeared in later Florentine architecture, in the work of Giuliano da Sangallo, Buontalenti, etc. The colossal proportions of the building are controlled by the design of the façade with its clear succession of modular units, which some critics have seen as an interpretation of Roman structures with a superimposed series of arches. Brunelleschi's modular conception was perceived by Vasari: "The doors are double, 16 x 8 *braccia*, the windows of the first and second stories resembling the doors in every respect. The vaulting is double... " The modular basis of the design explains how it was possible to enlarge the building in various subsequent periods without deviating from its original matrix; indeed, even in the 18th and 19th centuries this principle of order and regularity was accepted but interpreted in depth (in the projecting lateral wings), creating a stage-like, romantic effect. Although many additions have been made to the structure, the palace has never served as a model for other buildings.

The observer is immediately struck by the perfect calculation in the treatment of the wall plane with respect to the frontal view and of the distance between the viewpoint from below and the façade wall. Other major Florentine palaces were built with a corner view in mind, and therefore reveal a more volumetric conception. The façade of the Pitti Palace, on the contrary, seen frontally from the square, presents a simple homogeneous plane which yet evokes an impression of volume and of the occupation of space. The conception of the structure as a single plane is accentuated by certain features, such as the equal height of the floors, the use of equal windows for each floor and the use of the same rusticated blocks for the entire elevation. (The importance of these features is evident if we compare this building to Michelozzo's Palazzo Medici.) The original impression of the Pitti Palace as seen from a viewpoint at the bottom of the steep ascending plane of the square has in large part been lost because of alterations and additions which have been made since the 16th century. But we have not lost Brunelleschi's basic modular conception, nor the large-scale relation of the structure to the rest of the city, particularly the role of the façade, rising above and facing the Oltrarno, in subtle correspondence to Santo Spirito.

It is clear from Brunelleschi's work at the Palazzo di Parte Guelfa, from his project for Palazzo Medici and from the design for the Pitti Palace, that he intended to introduce into civil architecture a complex system of references to the surrounding urban context, in keeping with his conception of the city as an architectural unity.

Civic architecture of the 15th century, particularly of the first half of the century, was more traditional and more influenced by Gothic taste than contemporary religious architecture was. In fact, Brunelleschi's innovatory projects for the Palazzo di Parte Guelfa and for the Palazzo Medici met with strong opposition and failed to stimulate a cultural or typological evolution similar to that produced by his religious architecture.

It was difficult to repeat the remarkable synthesis of new and traditional ideas which Brunelleschi achieved in the design of the Palazzo di Parte Guelfa or of the Pitti Palace (note that he did not use the Classical orders). In fact, Michelozzo and others reverted to a more medieval conception, and Alberti's more intellectualized prototype, Palazzo Rucellai, more easily won acceptance.

Bibliography

G. C. ARGAN, *Brunelleschi*, Milan, 1955; P. SANPAOLESI, *Brunelleschi*, Milan, 1963; E. LUPORINI, *Brunelleschi, forma e ragione*, Milan, 1964; L. BENEVOLO, S. CHIEFFI, G. MAZZETTI, *Indagine sul S. Spirito del Brunelleschi*, in « Quaderni dell'Istituto di Storia dell'Architettura », Rome, 1968; H. SAALMAN (ed.), *The Life of Brunelleschi by Antonio di Tuccio Manetti*, University Park (Pa.) and London, 1970; H. KLOTZ, *Die Frühwerke Brunelleschis und die mittelalterliche Tradition*, Berlin, 1970; F. D. PRAGER and G. SCAGLIA, *Brunelleschi, Studies of his Technology and Inventions*, Cambridge (Mass.) and London, 1970; G. FANELLI, *Firenze, architettura e città*, Florence, 1973; I. HYMAN, *Brunelleschi in Perspective*, Englewood Cliffs (N. J.), 1974; E. BATTISTI, *Brunelleschi*, Milan, 1976; D. DE ROBERTIS and G. TANTURLI (eds.), *Vita di Filippo Brunelleschi di Antonio Manetti*, Milan, 1976; S. DI PASQUALE, *Primo rapporto sulla cupola di Santa Maria del Fiore*, Florence, 1977; C. L. RAGGHIANTI, *Filippo Brunelleschi, un uomo un universo*, Florence, 1977.

NOTE. *The author wishes to thank Nuova Vallecchi editore for permission to reproduce parts of the chapter on Brunelleschi originally published in G. FANELLI, Firenze, architettura e città, Florence, 1977.*

The author also expresses his gratitude to the architect Rindo Frilli, who organized the photographic campaign carried out by Mauro Sarri.